FATAL COLLISIONS

■

Robert Foster lectures in the History Department at the University of Adelaide, specialising in the history of Indigenous people in South Australia. His major research interests are European representations of Aboriginal Australians and the history of Aboriginal rights to land.

Rick Hosking was born in the Flinders Ranges and grew up on the west coast of South Australia. He lectures in the English Department at Flinders University, where he teaches literature topics, Australian Studies, Professional English and Creative Writing. He is currently working on a cook book and a book on John Lang, the first native-born Australian novelist.

Amanda Nettelbeck lectures in the English Department at the University of Adelaide. She publishes and teaches in the areas of colonial and contemporary Australian writing and autobiography.

Robert Foster and Amanda Nettelbeck are working on a biography of William Willshire, the notorious Mounted Constable who policed the central Australian frontier in the 1880s and 1890s.

FATAL COLLISIONS

The South Australian frontier and the violence of memory

Robert Foster, Rick Hosking
and Amanda Nettelbeck

Wakefield
Press

Wakefield Press
16 Rose Street
Mile End
South Australia 5031

First published 2001
Reprinted 2017

'The Legend of James Brown' originally appeared in *Australian Historical Studies*,
No. 111, October, 1998. 'Logic's Unexpected Celebrity' originally appeared in *History
in Portraits*, (eds. J. Simpson and L. Hercus) Aboriginal History Monograph no. 6,
1998. 'Regional History and the Rufus River Conflicts' originally appeared
as 'Mythologising the Frontier' in *Journal of Australian Studies*, no. 61, 1999.
The authors thank the editorial boards of those journals for permission to reproduce
those articles in this book.

Cover image *A Fight at the Murray*, W.A. Cawthorne, courtesy of
the Image Library, State Library of New South Wales
Designed and typeset by Clinton Ellicott, Wakefield Press

National Library of Australia Cataloguing-in-publication entry

Foster, Robert.
Fatal collisions: the South Australian frontier and the violence of memory.

Includes index.
ISBN 978 1 86254 533 5.

1. Violence – Australia. 2. Racism – Australia – History – 19th century.
3. Australia – History – 19th century. I. Hosking, Rick.
II. Nettelbeck, Amanda. III. Title.

305.800994

C

CORIOLE
McLAREN VALE

CONTENTS

■

PREFACE

■

The idea for this book originated in the discovery that the three of us –
scholars in the fields of History, English and Cultural Studies – had been
working independently on the same body of material and exploring
similar themes. We decided to combine our individual projects in the
belief that, together, they told a fascinating and important story, and
one that would be enriched by our different disciplinary approaches.
This is a story which takes place in that fluid zone where history,
memory and myth meet in popular consciousness, and its subject is
the way in which European accounts of frontier violence have been
mythologised over time.

While each chapter in this book tells a unique story, collectively
they form a narrative sequence: events examined in early chapters have
a bearing upon the way events examined in subsequent ones were
played out. However, this book is not intended to be a history of
violence on the South Australia frontier, but rather an exploration of the
ways in which the violence has been remembered.

Robert Foster, Rick Hosking and Amanda Nettelback,
Adelaide, 2001

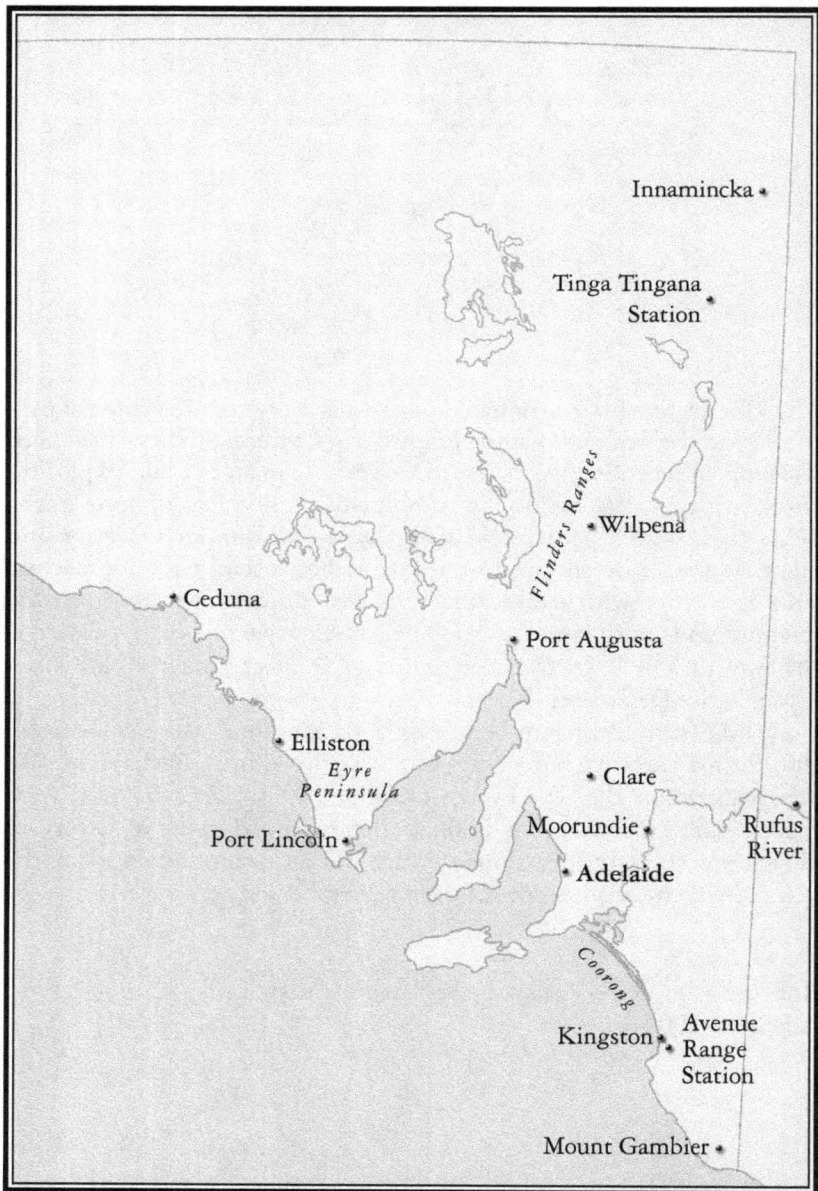

Map of South Australia showing main locations referred to in
this book.

INTRODUCTION: THE VIOLENCE OF MEMORY

■

The characters sketched in this story were . . . far from the settlements, surrounded by some of the fiercest of the native tribes of Australia, and entirely dependent upon themselves. It is not to be wondered at if, under these circumstances, deeds were committed at which humanity shudders. It is generally assumed that the blacks were the aggressors. No doubt they were so, by stealing sheep and cattle; but that was in retaliation for their country having previously been taken possession of, and in this respect it cannot be disputed that the white man was the aggressor.

Simpson Newland, *Paving the Way*, 1893

In 1849 James Brown, a pastoralist in the lower south-east of South Australia, was charged with shooting dead nine Aboriginal people: an old man, five women and three children. Unable to find witnesses, the crown dropped the case and Brown was released without trial, but few doubted his guilt. According to a local district magistrate, there was 'little question of the butchery or of the butcher'. Brown went on to become a wealthy landowner in the district, eventually entering the pantheon of South Australia's pastoral pioneers. A biography of Brown written in the mid-1920s made a brief reference to the events of 1849, noting that he was 'involved in a charge of poisoning a black-fellow, but emerged from the trial with a clean escutcheon'.[1] Why had the story changed so much: from shooting to poisoning, from nine victims to one, from never facing trial, to being found not guilty?

What forces were at play re-shaping the communal memory of this event?

This book is about the violence of the Australian frontier and the way it has been remembered in Anglo-Australian accounts of the past. In our study of six different frontier episodes, we explore how the memory of those events has been transformed over time. Our primary aim is not so much to uncover the 'truth' of the historical events – although what actually happened, as far as can be established, is important to our analysis – but rather to examine how the events have been mythologised. While these stories of frontier violence may have been mythologised, the violence of the frontier was no myth.

SOUTH AUSTRALIAN SETTLEMENT AND FRONTIER VIOLENCE

South Australians have long thought of their state as one that has been different in its treatment of Indigenous people. On the eve of settlement the colonisation commissioners in England wrote that 'far from being an invasion of the rights of the Aborigines', the new colony would be settled by 'industrious and virtuous settlers' who would protect them from the pirates, squatters and runaway convicts who infested the coast.[2] Yet the Act establishing the colony, passed two years before the commissioners wrote their report, made no mention of the Indigenous inhabitants and declared the region 'waste and unoccupied'.[3] What had changed was not the sentiments of the prospective colonists, but those of the British government. Shortly after the passage of the South Australia Act in 1834, a Whig government under Lord Melbourne came to power and the colonial office was now dominated by humanitarians. Men such as Lord Glenelg, Sir George Grey and James Stephens, who had been active campaigners against slavery, now expressed their concerns about the rights of Indigenous people. It was through their efforts that South Australia's colonisation commissioners were made to take the rights and interests of Indigenous people into account.[4] It is debatable whether the exertions of the colonial office had much effect – it was a long way, both literally and metaphorically, from the enlightened rhetoric of Exeter Hall to the realities of the Australian frontier.

The colonial office, concerned that previous colonial policy had been capricious and had given licence to the inhumane treatment of

Aboriginal people, insisted that they be regarded as British subjects.[5] Captain Hindmarsh, the first governor of South Australia, made this theme the centrepiece of his Proclamation speech in 1836. He told the colonists of his intention

> to take every lawful means for extending the same protection to the Native Populations as to the rest of His Majesty's Subjects, and of my firm determination to punish with exemplary severity, all acts of violence and injustice which may in any manner be practised or attempted against the Natives, who are to be considered as much under the safeguard of the law as the Colonists themselves, and equally entitled to the privileges of British subjects. I trust therefore, with confidence to the exercise of moderation and forbearance by all classes, in their intercourse with the Native Inhabitants, and that they will admit no opportunity of assisting me to Fulfill His Majesty's most gracious and benevolent intentions towards them, by promoting their advancement in civilization, and ultimately, under the blessing of Divine Providence, their conversion to the Christian faith.[6]

Hindmarsh's declaration that Aboriginal people were to be considered British subjects did not alter the realities of settler violence and Aboriginal resistance to invasion. A war was being fought which could not officially be acknowledged. How could a violent frontier exist between British subjects? This contradiction would lead to a frontier culture in which violence tended to be covert, and its representation clothed in euphemism.

At first, the colony that 'was to be different' did indeed appear to be so, with very few clashes between settlers and Aboriginal people in the first 18 months of settlement. The colonists proudly boasted of their good relations with the Aborigines, which they explained by reference to the 'good character' of the settlers and the alleged acquiescence of the original owners of the land.[7] In truth it was neither government policy nor the 'good character' of the settlers that accounted for South Australia's relatively peaceful early years; the Kaurna of the Adelaide plains were simply overwhelmed by the sheer weight and concentration of European settlement. The slow progress of surveys meant that it was not until the early months of 1839 that the settlers began radiating outwards from Adelaide.[8]

A series of dramatic events shocked the colonists out of their complacency. In 1839 shepherds Duffield and Thompson were killed on the outskirts of Adelaide. In 1840, the Brig *Maria* was shipwrecked on the southern end of the Coorong, near the present-day town of Kingston, and 26 survivors were killed by Aboriginal people. Attacks on overlanding parties bringing sheep and cattle into the new colony culminated in a series of bloody clashes on the River Murray in 1841. By the following year the isolated settlement of Port Lincoln was in a state of siege as Aboriginal owners of the country attacked most of the newly established pastoral stations.[9] At this early stage of settlement, when the population was still small and the economy struggling, the government responded to these challenges with large-scale punitive expeditions, convinced that displays of force were necessary to demonstrate European authority.

In this climate of crisis, the morality of dispossession finally became a topic of public debate. Writing in the *Southern Australian*, editor Charles Mann put forth the standard justification for dispossession:

> In our opinion, we have exactly the same right to be here, that the older inhabitants have. They at a remote, as we at a later period, were guided here by enterprise or accident. From the moment they arrived, until the present, they have not sought, and therefore not acquired as tribes a property in the soil – nor, as individuals, the ownership of things which grow or roam upon its surface. They have neither erected habitations upon it, nor pierced its bosom to make it minister to their support and comfort. Generation after generation, their thinly scattered tribes have wandered homeless over its fertile districts, unconscious or heedless of the treasures within them. The earth was made for man. We found the country in the state in which ages before the black people had found it – its resources undeveloped, unappropriated![10]

Responding to Charles Mann's appeals to legal and political theory to justify dispossession, a correspondent to the same newspaper put the claims of the settlers more bluntly:

> It is now in vain to talk about the injustice of dispossessing the natives of part of their territories, though it were granted that they ever possessed them; every one of us, by coming here, has, in reality, said that we either had such a right – or, not having the right, that we, at least, had the might, and resolved to exercise it.[11]

The writer invited any of those who believed they were unjustly taking possession of the country to leave on the next boat home. He rejected as hypocritical the claim that they were acting toward the Indigenous people according to 'higher motives', suggesting that 'our conduct toward them, will be, and has been, regulated upon the principle of expediency and self-interest'.[12]

By the mid-1840s the pastoral frontier began to advance rapidly into the interior, and as it did so the clever words of newspaper editors and the ethical dilemmas of evangelists became increasingly irrelevant. For settlers, who were a long way from Adelaide and often well beyond the range of police and other government officials, utilitarian concerns prevailed. Not only were they unconcerned about any rights to the land Aboriginal people might have had, they quickly came to view them as trespassers on European land. James Hawker, who established Bungaree station north of Adelaide, describes the attitude of the settlers as they were establishing their runs:

> The manners and customs of the natives were not known, and no attempt at friendly overtures were considered necessary towards them in the earlier settlement of the northern districts; in fact, they were looked upon as equally detrimental with wild dogs on a run. All means short of extermination were used to drive them away from the runs . . .[13]

Faced with Aboriginal resistance, those on the frontiers of settlement employed common strategies to secure the land. In the early phase of settlement, many agreed that it was good policy to keep Aboriginal people 'at a distance'. In his epitome of race relations on the frontier, explorer and sub-protector Edward Eyre encapsulates the attitude of a typical colonist setting up his station. Feeling isolated from help, his men dispersed over the countryside, and having heard dire accounts about the 'treachery of the savage' the settler:

> comes to the conclusion, that it will be less trouble, and annoyance, and risk, to keep the natives away from his station altogether; and as soon as they make their appearance, they are roughly waved away from their own possessions: should they hesitate, or appear unwilling to depart, threats are made use of, weapons perhaps produced, and a show, at least, is made of an offensive character, even if no stronger measures be resorted to.[14]

As long as Aboriginal people held the Europeans in dread, so the argument went, they would not be tempted to approach.

Some observers explained the high level of violence in the Port Lincoln district in the early 1840s as a consequence of the timidity of the settlers. The editor of the *Adelaide Examiner*, Dr Richard Penney, ascribed the behaviour of the Aborigines in the district to 'the lamentable negligence of the former settlers in allowing robberies to take place almost every week with impunity, and the want of courage displayed by others . . .'[15] The pastoralist John Bull, in reflecting on the violence in Port Lincoln and other districts, distilled the moral:

> where the blacks, having taken advantage of a few individuals venturing to occupy lonely places, have killed them, safety for succeeding parties has not been secured until a dread has been created in the minds of the offending tribe by speedy and severe punishment inflicted on the offenders and accomplices, and on those who sheltered them. It is a fact that cannot be denied that there has been no safety for the lives and properties of the whites until such a dread has been established.[16]

J.F. Hayward's account of his experiences as a pastoralist in the northern districts of the colony in the 1850s reflect most of these ideas. He claimed that his 'campaigns' against the Aborigines were a necessary and ordinary part of frontier life:

> In every case that I missed sheep I at once followed them, camping when no longer their traces were visible, and at dawn again at them, till I rescued my sheep or punished the thieves.[17]

In Hayward's words, Aboriginal people had to be 'chastised' or 'terrified'; otherwise there would be no end to the attacks on his stock and property. Eliza Mahoney, in her memoirs of the 1840s, uses the same euphemism of punishment to express the ordinariness of vigilante violence: 'a few of the energetic young men . . . gave the blacks such a punishment' after the disappearance of sheep 'that they never attacked in any force again'. 'We supplied a horse,' she adds, willingly confessing collusion in what was clearly considered to be a common and acceptable response to 'troublesome blacks'.[18]

In modern critiques of the frontier, Indigenous violence against the settlers is rightly described in political terms. Historians now recognise Indigenous violence as 'resistance' and portray their methods as 'guerilla tactics' against an invading force.[19] This was not usually the contemporary portrayal. Aboriginal people on the frontier were commonly described as 'annoying' or 'troublesome', and their attacks those of 'depredators', 'marauders' or 'plunderers'. Alternatively, their actions were dismissively interpreted as indicative of their 'savage' character. In other words the vocabulary used in accounts of frontier violence classed Indigenous actions as criminal or malicious rather than as political in character.[20] More serious violence in frontier districts was sometimes described as 'warfare', but this was the exception rather than the rule.[21] For the settlers to view Aboriginal attacks on life and property as resistance against invasion would have been to ascribe a level of social organisation and political organisation to Indigenous society that they were rarely willing to concede.

Violence by settlers against Aboriginal people often went unreported. On those occasions that it was reported, it was typically ascribed to ex-convicts or other unsavoury characters who were said to be drawn to the isolated and lawless boundaries of European settlement. Explorer and colonial bureaucrat Charles Sturt argued that settlers often established their runs with every intention of treating the Aboriginal people fairly, but 'it more frequently happens, that the men who are sent to form out stations beyond the boundaries of location, are men of bold and unscrupulous dispositions, used to crime, accustomed to danger, and reckless as to whether they quarrel, or keep on good terms with the natives who visit them'.[22] Writing of his experiences in the northern districts of the colony in the 1850s, J.F. Hayward claimed that his men were the 'offscourings of the colony, old lags or convicts, who had pitched on the farthest out-station to avoid being followed by police'.[23] While the owners of pastoral runs may have found these men objectionable, and expressed disquiet about their actions, they nonetheless employed them, presumably because they did the job that was expected. It is telling that the only European hanged for killing an Aboriginal person in colonial South Australia was an ex-convict, Thomas Donnelly. Donnelly's hanging in 1847 was held out as an example of the legal system's impartiality, yet it did little to alter the essential realities of frontier violence; indeed, it may merely have ensured that Indigenous deaths at settlers' hands became more covert.

While the Australian frontier witnessed large scale battles between Aboriginal people and Europeans, such as the clashes near the Rufus

River in 1841, the violence was typically localised and covert. Writing of Yorke Peninsula in the mid-1840s a settler noted how he always reported the killing of Aboriginal people to the police, but added that many 'bushmen came to grief by keeping things of this sort quiet'.[24] The truth of the matter is that many bushmen did keep 'things of this sort quiet', but very few came to grief. While inquiring into the murder of an Indigenous boy in the south-east in 1846, a local magistrate observed:

> It is impossible to get at the truth among the rest of the ruffians who infest the neighbourhood and I believe a wholesale system of murder has been carried on, which it is most difficult to obtain any evidence of.[25]

As historian Tom Griffiths observes, war on the Australian frontier did not fit the colonists' 'image of a war':

> Their experience was not of public violence against a respected foe, but more frequently a drama of betrayal, fear and disdain. A proper war would have dignified their violence, brought it out in the open and allowed them the romance of heroes and campaigns.[26]

The undeclared war of the Australian frontier produced a culture of secrecy, ensuring that much of what happened would be clothed in euphemisms, and the knowledge transmitted with all the accuracy of a Chinese whisper.

It is this very pattern of violence that makes it so difficult to make definitive statements about the number of Aboriginal people who died in South Australia's frontier wars. The number of European deaths is easier to establish. Henry Reynolds estimates that, Australia-wide, somewhere between 2000 and 2500 Europeans died 'in the course of invasion and settlement'.[27] This estimate is based on a number of detailed regional studies. Loos and Reynolds estimate that 850 Europeans and the allies died 'by spear and club' in Queensland between 1840 and 1897, Ryan gives a figure of 200 for Tasmania while Christie offers a comparable figure for Victoria.[28] Given the pattern of violence, Reynolds suggests a ratio of between five and ten Aboriginal deaths to every one European death – a total of about 20,000.[29] A detailed survey of the South Australian experience has yet to be undertaken, but based on a preliminary survey of colonial records we would conservatively estimate a minimum of about 80 European deaths,[30] which would indicate an Aboriginal death-toll of between 400 and 800 people. These estimates for South Australia are, however, highly speculative and will remain so until a detailed study is undertaken.

MYTHOLOGISING THE FRONTIER

A feature of national histories written in the era of 'White Australia', from the turn of the century to the 1960s, is the almost total exclusion of Indigenous people from the story. In his landmark *Boyer Lectures* of 1968, the anthropologist W.E.H. Stanner drew the nation's attention to this fact, which he termed 'the great Australian silence'. It was not something, he said, that could be simply explained by absent-mindedness, but was rather 'a structural matter'. It was as though the window through which we viewed the past had 'been carefully placed to exclude a whole quadrant of the landscape'.[31] Walter Murdoch's school textbook, *The Making of Australia*, first published in 1917, provides us with a typical view from this window. It begins with the statement that when 'people talk about "the history of Australia", they mean the history of the white people who lived in Australia'. The Australian Aborigines, writes Murdoch, might be of interest to scientists, but they are of no concern to the historian:

> He is concerned with Australia only as a dwelling place of white men and women, settlers from overseas. It is his business to tell us how these white folk found the land, how they settled in it, how they explored it, and how they gradually made it the Australia we know to-day.[32]

In the grand narrative of Australian history, Indigenous people were consigned to the shadowy margins.

This is less true of regional and local histories. In a recent analysis of commemorative local histories written by students in the 1920s, the cultural historian Chris Healy notes that Aboriginal people were generally discussed in their accounts, even when they were excluded from the students' own textbooks. These histories, he writes, were the 'product of informed local historical knowledge' and 'completely at odds with the received wisdom of a twentieth-century white historical silence'.[33] The nature of their inclusion, however, was a selective one, shaped by the interests and aspirations of those telling the story, and the story they most wanted to tell was that of the 'white folk' who 'found' and 'settled' the land – the pioneer.

The 'pioneer legend' emerged in the 1880s and 1890s at a time when the frontier, for most Australians, was becoming increasingly distant in both time and space. It was the pioneer who became the focal point for the nationalist nostalgia of jubilee and centenary celebrations. In the same period, the experiences of the men and women who 'paved the way' were being recorded and their stories, whether contained in local histories, fiction, diaries or personal reminiscence, became very popular in the late nineteenth and early twentieth centuries. Typical of such accounts are the biographical sketches which comprise Rodney Cockburn's *The Pastoral Pioneers of South Australia*, which the author hopes will

> serve as an inspiration to the men and women of South Australia who are now engaged in carrying on the pastoral industry under conditions infinitely more safe and felicitous than were faced with varying degrees of triumph and disaster by those who blazed the trail.[34]

At the heart of 'pioneer legend', writes J.B. Hirst, is the theme of 'subduing the land and battling the elements'.[35] The legend 'celebrates courage, enterprise, hard work, and perseverance; it usually applies to the people who first settled the land, whether as pastoralists or farmers, and not those they employed'.[36] While Hirst makes no reference to Aboriginal people in the pioneer legend, they are clearly visible in a variety of roles: as faithful servants, guides, workers in the pastoral industry, but perhaps most importantly, as adversaries who had to be battled in the process of 'subduing the land'. A passage from the Cockburn's biography of the west coast pastoralist Thomas Alfred Wilson is typical:

> It required the exercise of no little courage as well as determination against heavy odds on the part of the pastoralist to enter into occupation of this isolated region so far away from the homes of the white settlers and where the blacks who had always been very troublesome, were still, even in the sixties, a constant menace to human life and the sheep farmer's flocks.[37]

While Aboriginal people were often present in accounts of pioneering experience, they were 'put in their place', the stories involving them usually reshaped, in one way or another, to demonstrate the defining virtues of the pioneer.

The pioneer legend played a fundamental role in shaping the way in which Aboriginal people were portrayed in these accounts of frontier violence. It provided a framework which structured the nature of remembrance. Yet it is important to note that other forces were also at work. In thinking about the evolution of these stories, we need to be aware of the varied circumstances in which they were told, and the various forms in which they were recorded. In some accounts, for instance, we see the conventions of romance fiction employed to build tension, add drama or evoke pathos. In others, we see the storyteller overtake the story, the gothic elements of an episode so beguiling that they survive while other more prosaic details are lost. Few of the accounts we examine are 'oral traditions' *per se*, but many are written accounts of oral traditions, dependent upon the authority of 'I was told'. Yet these are oral traditions within a literate culture: the yarn spun by the camp fire may find itself in the memoir or the novel, but just as likely, the yarn-spinner has read the novel or memoir. In tracing the genealogy of these stories, we can observe how they evolve, how new elements are added while others are dropped, until they often bear little resemblance to the events they purport to describe. It is in this sense they can be said to have mythic or legendary qualities.

Each of the chapters in this book traces the way in which a specific event in the history of the South Australian frontier has been transmitted in, and transformed by, the folk-memory of the South Australian community. The six frontier stories explored here took place across the colony during the nineteenth century, from the south-east to the west coast and from the southern Flinders northward to the Queensland border. While by no means covering the extent of the violence that occurred, or is remembered, they are representative of the ways in which the violence of the frontier has been mythologised.

Most importantly, this is a process which depended upon the silencing of other voices, most crucially Indigenous voices. Indigenous accounts of the same events have always existed, but Europeans have rarely listened to them. That perspective – the other side of the frontier – would of course have been antithetical to the pioneer history they were producing. This is not to say, however, that these accounts were immune from dissent or doubt. Disquiet and unease are apparent in many and suggests two conflicting community preoccupations: on the one hand, a pride in the deeds of those who 'paved the way', and on the other, an enduring anxiety about the implications of the colonial process. Given this contradiction, the process of mythologising the violent frontier has never been, and perhaps never can be, settled.

RECONSTRUCTING
THE *MARIA* MASSACRE

∎

In July 1840, some two dozen settlers (historical records suggest between 24 and 26) survived the shipwreck of their brig *Maria*, which had been travelling from Adelaide to Hobart, on a reef south of the Coorong in South Australia. They apparently walked safely ashore and began the trek back towards Adelaide. Shortly afterwards, news reached Adelaide that the entire party had been killed by members of the Milmenrura clan, a group of the Ngarrindjeri people.[1] In the new South Australian colony, this was the first time that Indigenous people reacted to European intrusion with large-scale violence; the event figures as the largest murder of Europeans by Indigenous people in Australia's colonial history.

The colonial government was then under its second governor, George Gawler, and he faced a difficult problem. Outraged feelings in Adelaide and the risk that settlers might take revenge into their own hands produced pressure on him to respond to the murders quickly and decisively. Yet the Milmenrura could not be brought to trial: there were no surviving European witnesses to the murders, and the evidence of Indigenous people was not admissible in court, on the grounds that they did not understand the nature of an oath (this was to change several years later, in 1849). Under the Proclamation of the colony all Indigenous people within the territory of South Australia were declared British subjects, giving them (at least in theory) the full protection of citizenry rights. Gawler's difficulty, then, lay in determining how justice could be seen to be served against a people who, under colonial law, were considered to be British subjects but who, in common practice, were considered to be a 'hostile tribe, that is . . . *a nation at enmity with her Majesty's Subjects*' (original emphasis).[2] In this respect the

O'Halloran's Expedition to the Coorong August 1840,
John Michael Skipper, oil on canvas, 63 x 83.7 cm,
Art Gallery of South Australia

'Pilgaru' – two natives hung for murder, September 1840,
E.C. Frome, watercolour on paper, 11.1 x 19 cm,
Art Gallery of South Australia

case of the *Maria* murders exposed a fundamental contradiction in the colonial mindset: that Indigenous people could be considered to be British subjects when they 'acquiesce in, and acknowledge a friendly relation with us'[3] and a separate nation 'at enmity' with Britain when they did not.

Gawler's way of handling this contradiction was to declare the case 'beyond the limits of ordinary British justice' and to proceed 'on the principles of martial law'.[4] He sent a police party to the Coorong under the command of the new police commissioner, Major Thomas O'Halloran. O'Halloran's extraordinary instructions were to enforce summary justice without trial: specifically, to identify if possible an arbitrary number of the murderers (up to three, and in the event two) and to hang them on the spot.[5]

O'Halloran's instructions were duly carried out in an elaborately formal but emotively symbolic ceremony: a ti-trees gallows (the pulleys carted all the way from Adelaide) was constructed over the grave site of the murdered Europeans and two Milmenrura men, chosen on hearsay, were hung in the sight of the captive members of their clan. O'Halloran's journal records that although all in the police party regarded the hangings as proper and fitting punishment, the mood of his men was subdued; no one found any great satisfaction in the awful proceedings.[6] E.C. Frome's sketch *'Pilgaru'*, one of a series of sketches drawn at the Coorong soon after the events, depicts a grotesque detail which O'Halloran also mentioned in his journal: the gallows being too low on the sandhills to allow an adequate drop, a soldier hurriedly had to scrape away a hole beneath the men's dangling feet. The Indigenous audience to the hangings were then instructed by O'Halloran 'ever to remember this day, and to bring their relatives and children to the spot that they might all see how the white man punished those who murdered any of his tribe'.[7]

Although the hanging of the Milmenrura men undoubtedly satisfied many in the colony, it raised a great sense of disquiet in others. Interestingly, Gawler's use of martial law against Indigenous people sparked more response than the murders of two dozen Europeans had done, and initiated a broader debate about the extent and limit of British law, and the application of that law to Indigenous people. These issues took up considerable space in the colony's newspapers and continued well into the next year. The fledging society of European settlers was divided by the event, the tone of correspondents' letters ranging from absolute approbation to utter outrage over the hanging of the Aboriginal men. The ripples caused by the hangings were felt not only in the colony but also in Britain, where the Aboriginal Protection Society expressed horror at Gawler's action and British law officers suggested that Gawler and O'Halloran could be open to the charge of murder (though such charges were never made). Gawler's recall to London because of his government's over-expenditure was probably decided before news of the event reached the Colonial Office, but his action over the *Maria* massacre was thought by many in the colony to be the essential cause of his replacement by George Grey the following year.

Gawler acknowledged the problematic nature of bringing British law to bear upon Indigenous populations when he noted in a minute to his council a month after the hangings that Indigenous and European cultures represented the antipodes of one another, and that 'it is not an easy thing to make antipodes meet'.[8] Yet he defended his use of 'expedient' action on the grounds that *'in the same proportion that the full protection and privileges of British subjects are accorded to savages . . . in that very same proportion are the natural born subjects of Great Britain deprived of the protection which is their especial birthright and privilege'* (original emphasis).[9] In other words, although British law accorded equal rights to all those under its jurisdiction, in practice those rights applied conditionally to Indigenous people: that is, when the 'especial birthright and privilege' of Europeans was threatened.

This defence of martial law on the grounds of expediency was certainly supported by many in the colony but was also hotly reproached by others over the following months. Predictably, there were correspondents to the newspapers who not only supported expedient bends in constitutional law but also appealed to the moral principle of 'an eye for an eye'. 'If there be any cause for regret in his Excellency's late proceedings,' wrote one, 'it is, I think, that instead of hanging two, he has not hung a number at least commensurate to that of our slaughtered fellow countrymen.'[10]

Others expressed alarm at a conditional interpretation of their own law. The *South Australian Register*'s editor George Stevenson used the newspaper's editorial space on several occasions to criticise the government's position. Though he did not cast doubt on the moral grounds of punitive action, Stevenson considered the hangings to be a breach of British law. He quoted from Governor Hindmarsh's Proclamation of

1836 in order to argue: 'Whether the natives themselves can be bound by the proclamation in question, or whether they recognize or value the title of English subjects, may admit of argument; but the Government, at least, is bound by its own act.'[11] When Gawler suggested that in the colonies 'aggressive' natives, like 'atheists, idiots, and young children' in Britain, were debarred from certain privileges of British subjects,[12] Stevenson retorted that 'an atheist or an idiot is [no] less under the safeguard of the law than the best Christian or the most sane man; and if . . . the native inhabitants of a British province, are, by the very extension of British dominion over their territory, British subjects, we have established their right conclusively to those immunities and privileges to which in that character they are entitled as fully and legally as the most undoubted English-born subjects of the Crown.'[13]

Many of the *Register*'s correspondents agreed. '*Expediency*,' wrote one, 'is a plea from which the mind revolts. What limits can be assigned to the exercise of power governed by expediency?' No man's life, he argued, whether that 'of a British subject, or a savage native – can be taken away on *the moral belief of his guilt*, and in the proclaimed absence of "all legal evidence of crime".'[14] In a letter to her brother George Harris on 27 December 1840, Mary Thomas, one of the earliest British colonists to arrive in South Australia, was unreservedly critical of Gawler's instructions. The action, she wrote, entailed 'a most flagrant breach of the laws and constitution of England' as well as an assumption of governmental power 'which even the Sovereign does not possess'. Anyone, she warned, would be 'at the mercy of any Governor, who, out of caprice or spite, may think fit to issue orders either to destroy their property or affect their existence'.[15] (Her moral stance on this issue may have been affected by a degree of political opportunism. Mary's husband, Robert Thomas, was the printer of the *Register* newspaper and Gawler, antagonised by the *Register*'s criticism of his punitive action, had recently taken the government's printing commission from the *Register* and placed it with the rival *Southern Australian*. In the same letter expressing outrage at Gawler's action, Mary vents her commercial grievance, complaining of a reduction of up to £1800 in annual income from the loss of government printing.)

Other colonists articulated a belief that the killings had been motivated by European behaviour, creating the possibility for a moral, rather than merely legal, query of the government's action. Richard Penny, the surgeon who accompanied the expedition to the site of the massacre, deplored the murders of the shipwrecked Europeans but nevertheless suggested that the Milmenrura people were motivated not by innate ferocity but by genuine grievance. 'The natives declare,' he said in a public lecture the following year, 'that they fished for them, found them water, and carried their provisions – and that, on arriving at the spot where their territory ended, they were refused the reward of blankets and other things [promised], as the party insisted that they should take them on to Adelaide . . . – this being the case, the natives began to help themselves, which being resisted, ended in the whole being overpowered and killed.'[16]

A correspondent to the *Register* in 1840 suspected a more familiar provocation of Indigenous grievance, speculating that sexual abuse of Indigenous women by the *Maria*'s crew provided a plausible, and certainly not unprecedented, reason for the deaths. Recalling the publicity surrounding the warm hospitality that the Milmenrura people had showed only two years earlier to the shipwrecked victims of the brig *Fanny* off the same coastline – an example of goodwill between different peoples which was jeopardised only by the crew's 'loose conduct . . . with the native women' – he implied that responsibility for Indigenous aggression usually lay at the feet of injudicious and violent Europeans, who in the history of interaction with Indigenous people had provided 'numerous illustrations' of 'improper interference' into indigenous life and laws:

> There has seldom been an arrival by land . . . which on its first reaching Adelaide, did not bring some tale of boasting and butchering the natives on the way. There are few in Adelaide who have communicated with the degraded ruffians in driving stock to this country, who have not heard them vaunt of their exploits in shooting or 'peppering' the natives in their route.

If, he concluded, 'there was no offence to them by the passengers of the *Maria*', the Milmenrura were in all likelihood enacting the 'retribution' to which the behaviour of 'their civilized white brethren' would have led them.[17]

This correspondent's speculation on the cause of the massacre has been corroborated by an explanation in Ngarrindjeri oral history which was given to the anthropologist Norman Tindale in 1934:

> Native tradition is fairly unanimous in its statement of the reasons
> for the killing of the *Maria* survivors. They were escorted safely
> from boundary to boundary, and safely passed on from clan to
> clan all the way from the vicinity of Lacepede Bay to the northern
> boundary of the Karagari clan . . . Here several of the sailors took
> a favourable opportunity of interfering with some native women.
> They were attacked and killed . . .[18]

Another Ngarrindjeri explanation of the events has been given
more recently. In 1988, the year of the bicentenary, Lola Cameron-
Bonney responded to a piece on the *Maria* episode in the *Australasian
Post*. She told how her great-great-grandmother was among the clan
which had first rescued the shipwreck victims: the Europeans were
safely passed along from clan to clan but, on the third handing-over,
conflict arose that led some young men to kill the Europeans. These
young men were tried by tribal elders and fatally punished for their
crime; the Milmenrura men who were hung by O'Halloran's party were
therefore innocent.[19]

The debate sparked by the *Maria* massacre and hangings continued
well into 1841 (and overlapped with responses to the next significant
crisis in race relations, the Rufus River clashes of that year). What
clearly emerges from this debate is that in the colony's early days,
responses to such vexed questions as the application of British law and
the constitutional rights of Indigenous people within their own, now
appropriated country – problems, as Gawler put it, of how 'to make
antipodes meet' – were complex, contested, and far from homogenous.

The *Maria* episode seemed to abate in the public consciousness
after 1841, but was brought into focus for the next colonial generation
with the publication, from about the late 1870s onwards, of reminiscences and histories of the foundational years. Often these narratives of
the early days were consciously prefaced by the writer's intention to pay
tribute to a pioneer past and the values with which that past had
become associated: self-reliance, struggle and perseverance, loyalty to
God and to the colonial endeavour. By the 1870s, when a legend of
the receding frontier was becoming established in writings about the
colony, the point of many foundational reminiscences was not so much
to highlight the social and political strifes of the foundation period but
rather to recall the difficulties and triumphs of European settlers in
the early years. Often such narratives were addressed to the following

generations of family or of the colonial community; their purpose was to record the past in a way that would honour the first generation of colonists. Many writers of published memoirs were landowners or significant figures in the colonial administration; they and their families were an essential part of the project of 'opening this now prosperous colony'.[20] In this sense, two kinds of story inhabit the colonial 'foundational' narrative: one is a personal memory of the past, and the other is a present, publicly circulating mythology about that past.

For writers such as these, the criticisms of Gawler's military action against the Milmenrura in 1840 can be dismissed as the complaints of 'armchair' humanitarians who had no direct knowledge of the frontier and its realities. Nathaniel Hailes was a journalist, businessman and local government official who published his memoirs of the early years in a newspaper serial between 1877 and 1878. His account of the *Maria* events concludes with the summation: 'A great deal was said and written at the time about the legality of the proceedings. Strictly speaking they were not legal [but] there are cases of emergency wherein adherence to strict law would inflict substantial injustice, and that was one of them.'[21] John Wrathall Bull was a prominent colonist who published his very popular memoir *Early Experiences of Colonial Life in South Australia* in 1878. In his account of the *Maria* story he refers to the hangings as a regrettable but necessary part of 'the course of settling this province': a course that entailed the 'irregular but humane' and ultimately 'necessary slaughter of blacks'.[22] Bull's reputation in his own day was as a humanitarian and a friend to the 'blacks',[23] but as a successful English colonist his approach to race conflict was pragmatic and patriotic, and he scorned those who criticised Gawler's military action as unfit to comment on the hard truths of pioneer life.[24] A similar tone pervades the 1882 *Reminiscences* of Alexander Tolmer, the sub-inspector of police who took part in O'Halloran's punitive expedition to the Coorong. The early criticism of the colonial government that was provoked by the hangings of the two Milmenrura men is dismissed in Tolmer's account as an 'unjust treatment' of the case by 'some persons miscalled philanthropists'.[25]

Nathaniel Hailes and John W. Bull go further in their approval of Gawler's punitive action. Both describe the hanging of the two men as a 'merciful' measure, in the sense that it dampened the passions of settlers who might take revenge into their own hands.[26] Here these writers seem to assume that their local readers – perhaps older colonists like themselves – will share the 'unofficial' understanding that unlawful violence against Indigenous people was an inevitable part of life on the pioneering frontier. The government's action against the Milmenrura is offered less as a military punishment, more as a form of tough-minded benevolence that 'protects' Indigenous people from further settler retribution.

In this sense these accounts tend towards historical closure, smoothing away the troubling aspects of the events. What they open up instead is the dramatic possibilities of literary narrative. A striking feature of many foundational memoirs is their use of the heightened, usually melodramatic, language of masculine adventure narrative. In his book *Writing the Colonial Adventure*, cultural critic Robert Dixon has argued that the novel of imperial adventure/romance emerged as a revived genre in Britain and its colonies from the 1870s.[27] Given that the genre of memoir in this period is not clearly written as factual 'history' but tends to conflate memory, historical event and fiction, it is not surprising that the foundational stories emerging in South Australia from about the 1870s often do represent events as though they were adventure stories. While each claims to present the 'truth', Hailes emphasises the military glory of O'Halloran's party (as well as his own act of 'patriotism on the occasion [in] lending [his] horse'),[28] Bull appeals to the 'thrilling pictures and sufferings' of colonial life,[29] and Tolmer focuses upon himself – his physical prowess, his bravery in pursuing the Indigenous 'villains' – as the heroic figure at the narrative's centre.[30]

A fictional dimension is particularly apparent in an account of the *Maria* episode that appeared in the *Adelaide Observer* in 1868.[31] A primary image in this story, borrowed from the stock characters of imperial adventure narratives, is that of the stealthy and treacherous 'native', against whom the courageous but defenceless shipwreck victims are rendered helpless. In the style of melodrama the narrative takes the reader through an imaginative reconstruction of the event, lingering on the innocent excitement of the women and children as they set off for Hobart Town, the terrors of the shipwreck and the tenacity of its survivors, the untrustworthiness and inherent malevolence of the 'savages' watching from the shore, and ultimately the 'horrible fate' awaiting the Europeans at the hands of the 'ferocious and bloodthirsty' natives, who in this version make a cowardly attack under the cover of night.[32]

> [T]hose savages were on the alert. They saw all that was going
> on; and when their preparations had been completed, they lost
> no time in falling with fiendish cruelty on the defenceless white
> people. To tell how savagely and with what bloodthirstiness they
> attacked the whole party one night in overwhelming numbers,
> and how completely they went through with their horrid work –
> sparing neither man, woman, nor child – would be only heaping
> up sickening details.

This version of this tale, with its powerful appeal to unspeakable
horrors (there are worse 'sickening details' about which it would be
unbearable to speak), includes an ending to the episode that rewrites
actual events.

> But these cruel murders were not unavenged. A Magistrate, with
> a body of police, was sent to the place, and . . . many natives who
> were found in possession of the property of the murdered people
> were executed on the spot. . . . [T]he punishment . . . was so
> severe that it evidently did them good; for when, soon afterwards,
> another vessel was wrecked in the same neighbourhood, they did
> not venture either to molest the sailors and passengers, or to touch
> a farthing's worth of their property.

In this particular version of popular memory, then, the 'punishment'
visited upon the Milmenrura was more violent than it really had been
('many natives . . . were executed on the spot'), and the imagined
severity of that punishment becomes the justification ('it evidently did
them good') for later, peaceable race relations in the region.

During the 1880s other features of nineteenth-century popular
culture entered 'reminiscences' of the *Maria* events. The handwritten
memoirs of colonist Henry Dudley Melville (intended for publication,
but remaining unpublished)[33] introduced a recurring feature of what
the Australian literary critic Kay Schaffer has called colonialism's 'dark
fantasy of otherness',[34] the 'captivity narrative'. In a memoir liberally
punctuated with accounts of frontier warfare between early pastoralists
and Indigenous parties, as well as with euphemistic references to
settlers' skill in putting troublesome 'darkies' 'out of sight',[35] Melville
presents the spectre – one already familiar in the public consciousness of
colonial Australia in the figures of Eliza Fraser and the White Woman
of Gippsland[36] – of sexual violation of white women by 'savages' and the

threat of miscegenation. As various literary critics have argued in the Australian context, the captivity narrative marks out a particular crisis for the imperial culture's sense of natural order.[37] For a world in which civilisation was demonstrated by genteel femininity and barbarity by 'base' male sexuality, the suggestion of sexual contact between white women and black men was profoundly unsettling.[38] All the colonial anxiety released by the very idea of such a crisis is contained in Melville's account – presented as first-hand information – of a surviving woman passenger held as a slave to the sexual appetites of a native 'chief':[39]

> The natives of our run were the tribe that had murdered the crew and passengers of the 'Maria' some nine years previous to our occupation . . . [I learned that] the women were not killed at the time the men were, one woman was kept by a chief for three months and in trying to effect her escape was overtaken and speared at the Murray mouth . . .[40]

The captivity aspect of Melville's account has a compelling parallel with the Ngarrindjeri oral history of the *Maria* episode documented by Tindale in 1934. Tindale records that '[i]n the native tradition' there is the account of 'one white girl [who] escaped from the scene of the massacre'; she was found by the clan of the Murray Mouth and rescued by the women. Despite suggestions of a potential husband for her no man wanted to marry her: 'all were frightened that her colour (a sign of mourning) might adhere to them'. Soon afterwards a 'party of police [O'Halloran's expedition?] approached in a whaleboat, seized her, and despite her cries and protests, took her away to Goolwa'.[41] Clearly, then, the account of a female survivor from the *Maria* is intrinsic in both European and Ngarrindjeri oral histories. However, in the colonial European and the Ngarrindjeri accounts, the body of the white woman itself holds quite oppositional meanings: in the pioneer memoir it is the key to (European) civilisation while in the Ngarrindjeri account it is the threat to (Indigenous) civilisation.

Eliza Davies, who had in her youth been a domestic employee in Governor Gawler's household, published in 1881 her 'life story', *The Story of an Earnest Life*.[42] By the time of its writing, she had travelled the world and spent many years living in Canada; her book is part memoir, part travelogue and part romance fiction, filled with the excitements and travails of cross-colonial adventures designed to thrill a late nineteenth-century readership. She provides a brief but melodramatic account of the *Maria* murders, which sits alongside another story – offered as truth but readable as fiction[43] – of her own narrow escape, shortly before the *Maria* killings and in the same region, from predatory 'savage' men and a fate that can only be alluded to as 'a thousand times worse than death'. Here, the fears of being sexually violated and of being cannibalised by bestial men merge when she and her female companion become lost in the bush and stumble upon a group of men:

> Thoughts as quick as lightning flashed through my brain; first I feared being killed and eaten; then, O horror! I thought they might not kill us, but what would be a thousand times worse than death, they might carry us away and hide us . . . Meantime one of these panther-like monsters came close up to me . . . and put his great horny hand and arm close to mine. His touch made my flesh creep. . . . The close proximity of his great jaws and gleaming teeth made me shiver . . . We were surrounded by these horrible-looking men, their mouths wide open, and their tongues hanging out of their huge jaws, as if they were ready to devour us . . .[44]

Nothing happens; in the story, this imagined drama is resolved by her own action as a quick-thinking and courageous heroine. In her book this story becomes a link to the *Maria* events by her personal 'certainty' that one of the hanged Milmenrura men was one of the beast-like men she had encountered, his 'huge' mouth with its 'thick lips' and 'gleaming teeth' adding to her fear that he was 'about to tear me to pieces and eat me'.[45] The cannibal motif is taken even further in her version of the *Maria* murders with the additional detail to the story that 'four [white men] were roasted and eaten, and five were ready to be cooked and eaten'.[46] In Eliza's account, the values of civilisation are upheld by 'the gallant major', O'Halloran, whose punitive expedition became the means of preventing the 'butcher[ing of] white men . . . since that time'.[47]

By the 1880s, then, the legal and moral questions about colonial process, which had been raised about the *Maria* episode in 1840 and 1841, had become largely unasked in the popular genre of memoir and reminiscence; instead, the story itself had become embellished by a range of motifs commonly circulating in colonial culture: the treacherous, man-eating savage, the figure of the captive white woman, the military glory of the punitive expedition.

Yet although this was a strong trend, it was never total; an element of disquiet about the consequences of colonial expansion – violence, dispossession – does emerge in other, contemporaneous narratives of the colony's history. One of these was written in 1880 by Christina Smith, a lay missionary who migrated to South Australia in 1839 and moved with her family to the largely uncolonised district around Rivoli Bay, in South Australia's south-east, in 1845. Her book *The Booandik Tribe of South Australian Aborigines*[48] records her life of contact with the Buandig people of that region. Unlike a writer like Davies, who draws in her memoir on a literary tradition of entertaining adventures, Smith sees herself as a kind of ethnographic historian. She offers her book as a 'memorial' to the Buandig people, blending a nostalgic romanticism with the principles of social Darwinism, according to which primitive 'purity' must sadly give way to the greater force of Christian and industrialised civilisation.[49] Yet for her time, Smith offers an unusually dissident perspective on European frontier violences. She not only expresses her distrust of settlers' accounts of Indigenous aggression, but attempts to provide Indigenous perspectives of frontier clashes.[50] In her brief account of the *Maria* event, the Milmenrura people are not the initiators of aggression, and one of the hanged men is referred to as 'murdered' by the whites.[51] Given that her book was published in Adelaide and would have been received by a local readership, her account must have seemed provocative, at least.

Another late nineteenth-century version of the *Maria* story that raises a sense of unease about colonial process is contained in Simpson Newland's historical novel *Paving the Way: A Romance of the Australian Bush*, which was first published in 1893 and was republished as a popular romance in many editions through to the 1970s.[52] Newland was a prominent member of South Australian colonial society. By the time *Paving the Way* was published, he had been a successful pastoralist, a member of parliament, the Treasurer of South Australia and the President of the South Australian branch of the Royal Geographical Society. Older South Australian readers would have recognised more than one story of frontier violence that had its basis in local history, and in these cases, Newland is subtly critical of settler behaviour towards Aboriginal people, particularly when beyond the redresses of the law.[53]

At first glance, *Paving the Way* is quite conventional as a colonial adventure romance. Published first in London, it was presumably written for, and received by, a popular readership in Britain and

Australia well versed in the genre of colonial romance fiction. The first three chapters provide a fictionalised account of the *Maria* shipwreck and murders, and in them the narrative features of adventure romance are piled one upon the other: we have a young and handsome hero, the aristocratic Roland Grantley, who alone will escape the murderous savages; his dying mother, who bequeaths to him the family fortune; a 'stout-hearted' captain, who with his last breath fights valiantly to save his passengers; a treasure buried in the Coorong sands (which, borrowing from another racial stereotype, is hidden by a greedy Jew). In describing the scene of the murders Newland takes every opportunity to exploit gothic images of the grotesque. Driven by 'the blood-frenzy and love of slaughter common to all the aboriginals of Australia', the 'savages' fall upon the defenceless party at nightfall, the flickering light of campfires rendering them 'diabolical in their hideousness', and their triumph is signalled over the mangled bodies of the Europeans in 'wild' and 'brutal' cries.[54] Newland also enlists the captivity narrative: two surviving female passengers are 'borne away' swooning to a fate that (as in Davies' story) can only be implied as 'a dreadful one'.[55] And Newland carefully preserves the purity of white femininity: as savage warriors fight each other to 'clai[m] their rights over the captured women', the captives' lives are 'mercifully' ended by quick blows from a waddy.

Yet despite Newland's exploitation of such colonial literary stereotypes, *Paving the Way* is in many ways critical of European responses to crises of race relations during the South Australian foundational period.[56] At the same time that he presents the *Maria* murder scene in images of frenzied Aboriginal 'blood-lust', Newland presents the European party – specifically the ship's crew – as provoking the attack by sexually abusing the Indigenous women:

> the whites shrank together but there was no demonstration of hostilities on the part of the [natives]. . . . [W]hen the Europeans were prepared to march a number of the blacks accompanied them, indicating . . . the best way. Most of the day the journey was continued in a most amicable manner but towards evening some of the white men straggled behind among the lubras or native women, against the express commands of the captain . . . [A] number of the sailors did not rejoin their party at all and the demeanour of the blacks had also changed. That the overtures of

his men to the black women were bitterly resented by the natives
became very evident to the commander and that night a watch
was set . . .[57]

When, several chapters later, Newland presents a fictionalised version
of O'Halloran's court martial and hanging of the Milmenrura men, he
emphasises the 'farce of judging [the blacks] by our laws'. In Newland's
version, Major Cuthbert (O'Halloran), lacking any other firm evidence,
reluctantly selects for the gallows the two 'most villainous-looking'
men of the clan, and afterwards 'unburden[s] himself' to Grantley on
the impossible contradictions of his duty.[58] The ironic chapter title,
'British Justice', could not have escaped 1890s readers.

In *Paving the Way* Newland uses the adventures of his single pro-
tagonist Grantley to represent a series of frontier clashes that took
place across South Australia during the 1840s, and although Grantley
emerges from the *Maria* killings as the novel's clearly marked-out hero,
his mantle later slips when he takes part in a fictionalised version of
the 1849 Avenue Range Station massacre, in which nine Indigenous
people were murdered by the station owner.[59] At this and other
moments in the text, the distanced voice of the adventure narrative
shifts to an attempt to render an Indigenous perspective, and even
becomes directly polemical in attacking the effects of European colonial
violence:

> In [the eyes of the aboriginal] the white man was the personifi-
> cation of ruthless, all-absorbing power; never satisfied without the
> whole of the country; before whom his people absolutely withered
> away . . .
>
> From the first colonization to the present time, no adequate
> reserves have ever been set aside for the unfortunate people whom
> we have dispossessed and all but annihilated. This is a black
> indictment to make, but the sting is in its truth. Those who have
> seen the process must unhesitatingly though reluctantly admit
> that the darkest stain on Australia's fair fame is her treatment of
> the aboriginal race. We found them a happy, healthy people and
> wherever we have come in contact with them, in less than fifty
> years we have civilized them off the face of the land . . .[60]

Certainly, Newland's novel celebrates the pioneer years in romance
form; at the same time, the ambivalence he felt about the days of pioneer

success (in another essay, he suggested turning over Younghusband Peninsula to the Ngarrindjeri[61]) is expressed – in remarkably modern terms – in the statement of intention he recorded in his posthumously-published *Memoirs*: he wanted *Paving the Way*, he wrote, to chronicle '[the blacks'] struggle against the white invader in the early days of British colonization in Australia'.[62] Most provocatively for his local audience, perhaps, Newland's historical romance blurs the lines between the 'villains' and the 'heroes' of the frontier. Such criticisms, though, could only work within the limits of the genre and the period of its popularity. According to the codes of colonial historical romance, Indigenous 'struggle against the white invader' could be perceived as noble, even as gruesomely heroic, but by the late nineteenth century that struggle must finally be seen – as in Christina Smith's pseudo-anthropological 'memorial' to the Buandig people – to have failed against the greater force of 'civilisation'.

Certainly, Smith's and Newland's narratives are important amongst late-nineteenth-century versions of the *Maria* episode in recapturing some of the vexed problems revolving around frontier violence, problems which had been expressed in the aftermath of the hangings in 1840 but were, to one degree, written out of most later reminiscences. At the same time, they need to be remembered in the context of the culture which produced them. They might express regret for 'the darkest stain on Australia's fair fame, . . . her treatment of the aboriginal race'; but that regret can only be felt after the unassimilable 'aboriginal race' has, in the late colonial imagination, retreated to the shadowy place ascribed to it by imperial history.[63]

REGIONAL HISTORY AND THE RUFUS RIVER CONFLICTS

∎

Archaeologist Colin Pardoe suggested in 1994 that the region around Lake Victoria on the upper Murray River might be described as 'the Aboriginal equivalent of Sydney – the democratic heart and hub of the pre-European continent, linking trade and cultural routes from all points'.[1] In the early 1840s European overlanders increasingly used it too as they travelled with livestock between neighbouring colonies. The *Maria* events were still occupying the newspapers when violence erupted in April 1841 between overlanders travelling to Adelaide from New South Wales and the 'Maraura'[2] people of the upper Murray district near Lake Victoria.[3] This would be the first of a series of violent encounters between the Maraura and overlanders during the coming months. The overlanders and the pastoralists back in Adelaide attributed the Maraura people's aggression to the desire for livestock; few recognised such attacks as attempts to defend country. It was becoming clear, as South Australia developed its own trade and stock routes in the further reaches of the colony, that the increase in European/Indigenous contact would bring the same kinds of violence that had plagued the other colonies.

That conflict on the Rufus River and the colony's response to it were to be just as contentious as the *Maria* events had been the previous year is apparent in the gaps between the official and unofficial records of 1841. The events themselves have been the subject of numerous historical analyses in recent decades, but are worth retelling in order to consider more closely the different ways in which they were discussed in the government despatches, newspaper reports and colonists' diaries.

In April 1841 an overland party led by colonists Henry Field and
Henry Inman was attacked by the Maraura people near Lake Bonney,
leading to the dispersal of 5000 sheep and 800 head of cattle, and
the death of at least one Maraura man.[4] George Gawler, now in the
last month of his governorship, took immediate action with the despatch of a combined police and volunteer party under the command of
Major Thomas O'Halloran to retrieve the lost property. The function
of the expedition was primarily peace-keeping, but the major's journal,
written *en route*, reveals his expectation of punitive action. Oscillating
between the determination to avoid violence and the anticipation of
dispensing it, O'Halloran expressed the commonly held sentiment
that only 'severe punishment' would be a deterrent to Indigenous
threats:

> I think it possible that [the Natives] may dispute our passage . . .
> should this prove the case I consider that I should be fully justified
> by every law human & divine in forcing my way through . . . I shall
> be careful not to be the aggressor in any way . . . tho the punish-
> ment ought to be severe to prove to them our power . . . I think
> that a severe lesson to this fierce tribe would greatly conduce to the
> preservation of life hereafter.[5]

The major's anticipation of an encounter was frustrated, however,
when the party was compelled to turn back by the news of Gawler's
recall to London. He would be replaced by the young former explorer
George Grey. For O'Halloran, the cancellation of the expedition was
clearly a disappointing blow: 'It is with extreme pain and regret that I
have been forced to return back to Adelaide when within 50 miles of
the place where Inman's Party were attacked but I have no other alter-
native as an old soldier than to obey His Excy's orders'.[6]

Frustrated by the return of the government-sanctioned expedition,
a volunteer party of settlers formed under the lead of Henry Field. The
publicly expressed purpose of this settler action was the recovery of
the lost stock, yet the private diary of one of the participants, James
Hawker, reveals a more confrontational intention: 'our only hope',
Hawker wrote as they travelled to the district, 'is that the blacks will
stand in order that we may show them the use of *good* firearms'.[7] As
Hawker hoped, a clash did eventuate between the Maraura and the
settlers, and although Field's report to the governor's secretary does not
directly mention any Indigenous deaths,[8] Hawker's diary reveals that

the settlers shot six to eight Indigenous men during the course of battle, and escaped with no serious injury to their own party. This retribution seems not to have satisfied their sense of injustice, however; having been forced to retreat without recovering the stock, the settlers considered the expedition to be unsuccessful.

The new administration of Governor Grey was now established in Adelaide, and when the news arrived in late May that another party, led by stockholder Charles Langhorne, was on its way overland, two publicly published appeals, one by a group of colonists and the other by the stockholder's brother, were made to the new governor for aid towards a third expedition.[9] In their appeal the colonists made it clear that their land interests were at stake: since, in their eyes, the civic duty of the police merged seamlessly with those interests, they petitioned the government to make available 'a strong police force, to aid a number of gentlemen who will volunteer their services for that purpose'.

Whereas Governor Gawler's response to the *Maria* massacre had been underpinned by the belief that quick punitive action, even if beyond the exact letter of the law, produced the best resolution to frontier violence, Grey's response to the current crisis was more wary and equivocal. For a start, he expressed suspicion about the colonists' suggestion that the police should be regarded as a security force to protect the interests and risk-bound enterprises of overlanders, as well as that non-uniformed volunteers with undeclared designs should move against the Indigenous population. He also doubted that the attacks on overlanders were unprovoked. In a despatch to Secretary of State Lord John Russell he noted that aggression from Indigenous parties was likely to be caused by the 'ill usage' they had received from past over-landers, and expressed his disapproval of stockholders who, 'actuated by the hope of the large profit which may be realised', put their commercial interests ahead of every other consideration, 'making war upon their own account . . . [with] the tribes amongst whom their route lies' and endangering those whom they engaged to accompany their stock.[10] The tone of his response to the petitioners in Adelaide was rather more diplomatic. Yet although he confirmed his commitment to the security and interests of the colony, he made it clear that 'if proprietors, for the sake of gain, will venture with their flocks and herds so far beyond the limits of the settled districts, they voluntarily encounter a risk' from which the resources of the government could not always be expected to rescue them.

The most forceful message of his letter defined for its readers the primary difference between Grey's and Gawler's responses to trouble on the frontier: all Aboriginal peoples, Grey wrote, held the same rights of British subjecthood as did all settlers, and that 'to regard them as aliens, with whom a war can exist, and against whom Her Majesty's troops may exercise belligerent rights, is to deny that protection to which they derive the highest possible claim from the sovereignty which has been assumed over the whole of their ancient possessions'.[11] That last phrase – 'their ancient possessions' – comes as close as was then possible to an acknowledgment of pre-existing native title, a title that in the colony's law was subsumed under, though never completely cancelled by, the assumption of British sovereignty. In his reminder of the government's legal, as well as moral, obligation to the Indigenous population, Grey was supported by the *Register*'s editorial of 29 May, which compared his response with Gawler's action of the previous year:

> It is with the greatest possible satisfaction that we direct public attention to the Reply of Governor Grey to the Memorial . . . Our satisfaction is certainly not lessened by the formal establishment by Governor Grey of those principles which we have advocated from the commencement of the province up to this moment, and the confirmation of our views in reference to the natives, which, in the case of the Milmenrura murders, we maintained in opposition to Governor Gawler and his partisans . . . What becomes now of . . . the right of a Governor to take her Majesty's native subjects prisoners, and then hang or shoot them without proof, trial, or conviction?[12]

Grey's insistence upon the principle of Indigenous subjecthood under the Crown was part of a larger and then-fashionable plan for the assimilation of Indigenous people to 'civilisation',[13] but in this instance the principle was clearly enlisted as a reproach and a warning to belligerent-minded settlers. He did sanction an expedition, but on strongly conditional terms. When it left for the Murray, again under the command of Major O'Halloran, it would be accompanied by Protector of Aborigines Matthew Moorhouse, whose role was to 'act as protector and counsel of the natives'.[14] No guns were to be fired, except when 'absolutely necessary' in self-defence.

O'Halloran's party set off from Adelaide with orders to escort the overland party to Adelaide but before they could meet, Langhorne's men and the Maraura had already clashed. Four stockmen had died in the fight, introducing into the series of events the precedent of European deaths. A number of Maraura men were also killed, but this information was absent in Langhorne's official report to O'Halloran and in O'Halloran's report to Grey, appearing only in Moorhouse's report.[15] White men's deaths – and, in accordance with Grey's orders, the impossibility of exacting revenge for them – brought a new level of frustration to the Rufus River tensions. The major's diary records his sense of anxiety born of impotence: the party's Indigenous interpreters were, he repeatedly worried, 'nothing more or less than spies', and the governor's check on the use of weapons forced him to accept, without the usual capacity of retribution, the 'mocking' behaviour of treacherous natives from the river: 'Much disheartened – . . . I much fear that our trouble of the day, in allowing these fellows to escape without injury will do much future Mischief & make them more bold & daring than ever – They must now laugh at and Despise us . . .'.[16] The party returned to Adelaide, having fulfilled its orders with the recovery of the stock but dispirited by the impossibility of exacting punishment and embittered by internal tensions.[17]

The fourth and last expedition started from Adelaide in August after Grey received a settler's appeal to send armed protection to William Robinson's overland party, which would soon pass through the contested territory on its way to Adelaide. The killing of four white overlanders during the last trip injected a new sense of urgency into the petition.[18] Again wary of what he took to be settler demands for military-style retribution, Grey hesitated to commit government resources to a cause which not only might 'involve alike the innocent and guilty, men, women, and children in its consequences' but also was 'a matter of private adventure, not of public utility'.[19] On this point, Grey might well have had the political fate of his predecessor Governor Gawler in mind: Gawler was recalled primarily because of his government's over-expenditure. Pressed a second time he agreed to endorse an expedition to the Murray, but this time with fewer men than on the last occasion and commanded not by a member of the force but by Protector of Aborigines Matthew Moorhouse. Sub-Inspector of Police Barnard Shaw would take second command. The expedition's 'main object', Grey wrote to Moorhouse, was to prevent a collision between Europeans and Aboriginal people; he felt assured that Moorhouse would let pass no opportunity of establishing friendlier relations between the two peoples.[20] Yet when the police party met Robinson's overlander party on 27 August, it was to learn that the overlanders had been attacked the previous day. The party had lost no numbers themselves but in defending the stock had killed five and wounded another ten Indigenous men.

Within an hour of this meeting, the 'severe lesson' that O'Halloran had expected to administer during the first, frustrated expedition took place. The police and overlander parties met a large Maraura group in a tense encounter on the banks of the Rufus River. Feeling vulnerable to imminent attack, Moorhouse abandoned attempts at mediation and gave up his command to Shaw. Without waiting for orders, the overland party opened fire, followed by the police party from the opposite bank of the river. Of the Indigenous group of men, women and children wedged between them, according to Matthew Moorhouse's report, nearly 30 were killed and many wounded.[21] Once again, other records cast doubt on the estimations of Indigenous deaths. In his memoir published in 1899, James Hawker wrote: 'in after years, when I was residing on the Murray and had learnt the language of the natives, I ascertained that a much larger number had been killed, for Mr Robinson's men were all picked marksmen'.[22] When the party returned to Adelaide in September, Grey called an inquiry into the massacre. The resolution of the bench of magistrates, moved by Major O'Halloran – conveniently enough, here in his role as justice of the peace – was that the party's conduct was 'justifiable, indeed unavoidable in the circumstances'.[23] The Major's role in deciding this resolution highlights the irony of a colonial administration in which military-style punitive actions could be understood as peace-keeping ones. In this way the conflict on the upper Murray frontier, which had dragged from April to August, was finalised in the colonial records.

The Rufus River conflict remained, at least in the publicly available records, a largely forgotton chapter of colonial race relations until the publication of John Wrathall Bull's *Early Experiences of Life in South Australia* 37 years later in 1878. *Early Experiences* proved to be a template for South Australian pioneer memoirs to come. In fact, despite its strong element of autobiography and adventure romance, *Early Experiences* was quickly received as a text of historical veracity, and remained so right through the twentieth century.[24]

Like other colonial memoirs offering an 'eyewitness' perspective on regional history, *Early Experiences* fulfils its author's declared intention to commemorate the pioneer culture of the recent past. In his preface to the first edition, Bull commends the book to 'the rising generation of colonists' in order that they should 'become acquainted with some of the hardships and dangers' faced by their forefathers and so take 'pride and satisfaction' in the potential of 'adding to the renown of our glorious Empire'.[25] This kind of appeal, which constructs the past as a bridge to the future, has a powerful theatrical dimension, particularly in the context of imperial history.[26] The self-conscious metaphor of history as a stage, on which the colonial actor 'blazes a trail'[27] towards a future of progress and success, was a common feature of retrospective assessments of the early pioneer years, particularly in commemorative narratives such as centenary publications of 1936.[28] The metaphor appears in the introduction to the first edition of *Early Experiences* by another well-known South Australian colonist, J. P. Stow. Stow offers an image of Bull as dramatist, creating a history that takes place on stage as a performance produced to educate and inspire future generations:

> The author's aim has been to relate striking incidents coming generally under his own observation in the early days of the province; to describe the struggles of the pioneer settlers, the misfortunes and disasters against which they contended, and the scenes in which they were actors . . . Many of the adventures Mr Bull describes have a great element of romance about them, and . . . cannot fail to be exciting and attractive reading.

Bull's interest in the literary potential of the frontier as a dramatic subject is visible in the ways in which he rescripted his son John's 1864 diary of an overland journey to the uncolonised north of South Australia. In a draft preface to a planned chapter on overland experience (which did not eventually appear in *Early Experiences*), Bull described his intention to select from John's diary 'such portions as give touching descriptions of the suffering and fatigues almost unprecedented which he and his small parties endured'.[29] Yet what Bull calls a process of selection was in fact a process of revision. He revises John's often plodding and prosaic diary to give it the dramatic momentum of an adventure narrative, enhancing the journal with some of the colonial romance story's most popular stereotypes: the heroic and resourceful white explorer, the stealthy and treacherous 'native'.

In *Early Experiences*, he brings a similar understanding of narrative drama and effect to the 1841 Rufus River records. He wasn't a part of any of the expeditions, and his account of them is compiled from the documents available to him: the unpublished expedition diaries of Major O'Halloran and James Hawker, to which he had private access, and newspaper records.[30] In Bull's hands, most of these materials are altered in ways that unify and celebrate the history of a receding frontier and the heroic substance of its European actors. The vexed quality of those original records – the inconsistencies, anxieties and conflicts of interest which they reveal – is largely smoothed away by Bull's pen. Instead, his focus is on the drama of the frontier. While the government records of 1841 show some concern with the cause of the conflict,[31] Bull's account does not, to any significant degree. Bull's lack of interest in the circumstances producing conflict is surely not due to a failure on his part to acknowledge European injustices against Aboriginal people; his book does, in fact, several times express disgust at the violence of European settlement.[32] His concern with drama rather than with cause is, more fundamentally, a feature of the genre in which he wrote: a genre which aimed to commemorate the valour and the sufferings of pioneers in an age of emerging national pride, when 'white knowledge' about Indigenous decline was based on a social Darwinist ideology of the 'dying race' rather than on a recognition of colonial culture's responsibility.[33]

Bull's literary endeavours went further than mere stylistic alterations to the accounts in newspaper records and diaries. In one instance, he took a particularly compelling story about a dead overlander's faithful dog, which kept watch over his master's body, from one source and attributed it to another, with elaborated detail, presumably in order to enhance narrative continuity and effect.[34] True to the promise of his chapter introduction to depict 'the sufferings endured by pioneers', Bull injects into the diaries a self-conscious stoicism. Where doubt or even self-irony appears in the original diaries, it is excluded or modified in Bull's account. While citing Hawker on the volunteers' expedition, for instance, Bull leaves out Hawker's rather uninspiring entry on 11 May: 'Took the wrong track, had some difficulty in finding the main one'. Also left out is Hawker's admission that the Maraura party actually allowed the much smaller European party an avenue of escape: '[the] chief leader of this party . . . motioned to us to go away which hint we were very glad to take'. On the other hand, sentiments of a more rousing kind are added to Hawker's diary: 'We rallied three times, and kept our adversaries in check'.[35]

Predictably, Hawker's prosaic acceptance of conflicting interests on the frontier is, like that of Bull's son, revised in accordance with the literary stereotypes of pioneer stoicism and (as its counterpart) Indigenous savagery.[36] Where Hawker describes the Maraura 'army' as a force equal to their own, Bull describes a demonised enemy, infusing Hawker's account of the suspenseful moments before the conflict with an element of gothic horror:

> Hawker: We came into a small flat . . . in which between two and three hundred blacks were collected ready to receive us (several of them were painted with white and red which they do when they are going to fight.) Capt. Field ordered us immediately to form into line but several of the horses being restive from the yelling of the natives we found it impossible to do so. The moment we halted one of the natives threw a Spear into the ground this was immediately followed by one at Capt. Field which luckily glanced off a tree. Capt. Field shot the man who threw this Spear dead and some more shots were fired with success.

> Bull (citing Hawker's diary): 'The natives when met were in their war paint, with white bars on their bodies and limbs, giving them the appearance of skeletons. It was found that the horses would not steadily face them, the blacks also yelling in the most hideous manner.'

Bull's account of the third expedition, which absorbs two chapters, is both the most literary and the most obviously polemical of the chapters devoted to the Rufus River events. A new factor had entered the story: although a number of Indigenous men had met their deaths in encounters with Inman's and the volunteers' parties, the third expedition saw, for the first time during these events, the deaths of Europeans. Whereas the outraged tone of the colonists' memorial to Grey of 1841 requesting the expedition was based on the perceived threat to their land interests, Bull, with the benefit of hindsight, infuses his account with a more potent form of moral injustice: the deaths of white men. The first of the two chapters to deal with this expedition is marked by a strong sense of narrative suspense, leading readers inexorably through O'Halloran's travels towards the revelation of the stockmen's deaths, and reserving the climax of the battle, as well as O'Halloran's discovery of one 'shockingly mangled' European corpse, for the next chapter.[37]

When, finally, the body's discovery is described (although attributed to 'the Major's diary', the description is in fact compiled from both O'Halloran's and Hawker's diaries[38]), Bull adds details that are absent in the original accounts – 'masses of mangled bone, brains, and congealed blood'[39] – to excite further horror in the minds of his readers, and exploits the natural pathos lent to the scene by the fact (recorded in several accounts of the time) that the dead stockman's dog remained at the body's side.[40]

> By the side of the body of Martin was seen a faithful bulldog named Bulcher, which appeared to be wounded. The poor brute, alarmed at the approach of the police, took to the water, giving vent to a most piteous howl, which none of the hearers would be likely to forget. The rescued men said the dog had fought the blacks nobly, and was supposed to have been killed.[41]

Bull's account of the aftermath of the body's discovery is drawn from Hawker's diary, but with the addition, again, of the motif of Aboriginal treachery. Whereas Hawker's entry for 23 June simply notes that amongst an Indigenous group swimming in the river were those 'who told us that the sheep were alive (&c)', Bull's citation is more provocative: 'The natives who had promised to give up the sheep were amongst the swimming niggers, thus proving their treachery'.[42] Bull's account does not mention that more Maraura were killed in the battle than overlanders.[43]

The edge of narrative drama in Bull's account is combined with a polemic against Governor Grey, whose policy of non-violent intervention provokes Bull's contempt. While the *Register* in 1841 appealed to colonists for a moderate response to the crisis of race relations on the Murray,[44] Bull's account a generation later is fuelled by a sense of outrage, in particular at Grey's refusal to sanction the use of guns. Whereas he condones Governor Gawler's actions in the Milmenrura case,[45] Grey's policy on race relations is condemned by Bull as a 'weak, tampering policy' (' – peace officers to meet victorious blacks with spears in their hands!', he writes contemptuously[46]). He concludes with a declaration that, despite its appeal to the language of equality, reason and moral authority approves the use of force to protect colonial interests: 'it should have followed that subjects of whatever colour found in arms, and after committing such crimes as these had, should have been promptly treated as subjects in revolt, and have been dealt with accordingly, constables' staves being left at home'.[47]

This simplification of complex issues is also apparent in Bull's version of Grey's response to the memorialists' appeal for a third expedition. The governor's response had contained three critical issues which become blurred in Bull's account. First was Grey's point that 'rights' of colonists to retaliate against Indigenous 'outrages' do not in fact exist except in the wrong-headedness of some colonists' 'excited feelings'. Although Bull faithfully repeats Grey's refusal to accept belligerent *actions* against Indigenous peoples, he naturalises, with his contempt for Grey's policy, the existence of belligerent *rights*; in fact these rights are assumed at other points of his narrative in his distinction between the 'wilful' (that is, unjustified) and 'necessary' (that is, justified) killing of Indigenous people in the course of colonial settlement.[48] Second was Grey's insistence that Indigenous peoples were due the legal rights that subjecthood under the Crown entailed. This point is effectively sidestepped by Bull with the phrase 'subjects in revolt': the state of revolution – caused, the phrase suggests, by Indigenous aggression against the now 'natural' occupiers – allows for punitive actions not normally sanctioned in a state of civil peace. The third point of Grey's response to be written out of Bull's account was that government resources could not be held captive by the private interests of entrepreneurs. Although softened by his reassurance that he was aware of the importance of 'an easy and secure line of communication' between South Australia and neighbouring colonies, Grey made clear his disapproval of those who, 'for the sake of gain', travelled in small numbers into uncolonised territories and (as he suggested to Lord Russell) provoked war with their Indigenous inhabitants. In Bull's account, Grey's warning to overlanders about injudicious behaviour on the frontier is rewritten as prompt support: the governor, he writes, 'expressed his readiness to promote the objects in view so far as the means at his disposal would permit'.[49]

Bull's account of the last expedition and the resulting massacre is anti-climatic after the previous chapters: in the scheme of his narrative, the third expedition, with its striking literary potential (the dead stockman, guarded by his faithful dog; Aboriginal treachery and outrage) is the climax of the drama, and the killing of some 30 Maraura men, women and children takes the place of the after-effect of that drama. His version of the fourth expedition and massacre is compiled from Moorhouse's first report and extracts from the subsequent inquiry. These extracts are framed by Bull's own evaluative summary, which

interprets the massacre as not only manoeuvred by the Maraura themselves ('a conflict took place, when the little army of blacks *placed
themselves* between the two parties . . .'), but also due to them ('. . . and
advancing to attack at length met with their deserts').[50] In deflecting
responsibility for the massacre from the Europeans who pulled the
triggers to the Maraura themselves, Bull is in tune with the findings of
the official inquiry. When it closed on 22 September 1841 the bench
of magistrates carried Major O'Halloran's motion 'that the Europeans
on that occasion did not act with unnecessary severity against the
natives *when obliged to fire upon them*'.[51] Yet when he claims that 'no
subsequent censures were uttered or published' after the massacre,[52]
Bull is not quite right. Writing to Grey from London in May 1841, the
Colonial Office's Lord Stanley made it clear that although he accepted
the likelihood of the Aboriginal party's 'hostile intentions', he found it
reprehensible that Robinson's group fired without orders, and that the
firing continued at length upon people attempting to escape.[53]

The massacre also had its controversial representation in two
(undated) paintings by the South Australian artists S.T. Gill and
William Cawthorne. Gill's painting captures the self-justifying mood
of the 1841 inquiry, but also goes further, portraying an embattled
police party keeping at bay the aggressive Maraura, who attack not
only from the river but also from hidden positions behind bushes and
trees. (It is possible that in this painting Gill conflated two episodes:
the volunteer party's May expedition, in which the colonists found
themselves surrounded by the larger Indigenous party and beat a hasty
retreat, and the massacre of the Maraura on the river bank by the police
and overland parties on 27 August.) Cawthorne's painting, in contrast,
illustrates a less heroic scene closer to that conveyed by Moorhouse's
report: a group of Aboriginal people, trapped on the river bank between
the two European parties, and falling under the gunfire that is aimed
directly at them.

In written form, however, Bull's account of the Rufus River conflicts remained the most detailed of colonial accounts, and in the years
following its publication *Early Experiences* became an inspiration for
other South Australian foundation memoirs. That Alexander Tolmer
intended his 1882 *Reminiscences* to have the popularity accorded to Bull's
book is indicated, somewhat churlishly, in his preface: 'Shortly after the
publication of 'Early Recollections and Experiences of Colonial Life'
[sic], by Mr J.W. Bull, I was repeatedly urged by friends to write my

A Fight at the Murray, n.d., W.A. Cawthorne, Mitchell Library

Engagement with Aboriginals at Lake Bonney, River Murray,
27th August 1841, T.S. Gill

own reminiscences, instead of devoting my time to assist other authors.'
As a member of O'Halloran's first thwarted expedition, Tolmer had
first-hand experience of the punitive action on the Murray, unlike Bull;
yet his account of the Rufus River conflict – written nearly 40 years
after the event – adopts the same structure used by Bull and even
directly copies Bull's opening paragraphs.[54] James Hawker, whose
1841 diary of two of the expeditions had been a primary resource for
Bull, also closely follows the pattern of Bull's account in his similarly
named memoirs *Early Experiences in South Australia* (1899). The result,

by the turn of the century and arrival of Federation, was the creation of a cohesive and circular foundational history, one which became the source for twentieth-century historical accounts and smoothed over the disquieting ambiguities and ambivalences of earlier colonial records.

This was, inevitably, a foundational history which drew on and reflected the dominant features of late nineteenth-century popular thought, features which established a structure for the imaginative constitution of South Australianness. While many commentators of the foundation years were quite aware of the direct relationship between the practices of colonialism and destruction of Indigenous cultural life,[55] by the late nineteenth century this awareness was softened by the racial fatalism that social Darwinism allowed. Consistent with this aspect of contemporary thought, Bull's narrative simultaneously acknowledges and dismisses the settler society's responsibility for what he calls the 'disgrace' of Indigenous 'destruction'.[56] While he acknowledges frontier violence against Indigenous peoples as a real part of the settlement process, that violence is rendered insignificant by appeal to the idea of 'natural', even divine, law:

> The question of the displacement of an aboriginal race has always been attended with great difficulties, but is one of those necessary processes in the course of Providence to bring about the improvement of the human race and the promised latter days. . . . [T]he introduction of civilised habits seems to be fatal to their continued existence, independently of the vices and diseases we have brought among them.[57]

The late nineteenth-century view of the decline of Indigenous life as a regrettable 'necessity', which disconnected the settler society from responsibility for its violence, is again enlisted by Bull to endorse the local foundational myth that South Australia's process of settlement was relatively bloodless:

> It is a sad reflection that the white man, in seeking to occupy the countries the aboriginal races have previously wandered over, should have been under the necessity of taking their lives; but I do without hesitation assert that in South Australia the instances of wilful and unjustifiable destruction of them have been few in comparison to the cases of necessity.[58]

Early Experiences became central to the way in which Indigenous/ European conflict became incorporated into South Australia's foundational mythology, but Bull's narrative is not without its own ambivalences. Given his justification of the Rufus River massacre and other killings as cases of 'necessity',[59] one might think that Bull would not feel the need to say more. Yet despite his own reputation as an ambitious and successful colonist,[60] the chapter following his account of the massacre reveals a nagging sense of doubt about the appropriation of Indigenous land in aid of unfettered colonial expansion. According to his son, Bull enjoyed the reputation of maintaining good relations with local Indigenous communities,[61] and while *Early Experiences* justifies punitive action as a response to Indigenous resistance, it also imagines a program for the expansion and improvement of Indigenous land tenure.[62] Yet in the end, the degree of remorse marking Bull's narrative ('We had been received as friends, and now where are the original lords of the soil'[63]) is less than his commitment to the purpose and future of empire. In a direct address to the generations of that future, he advises: 'there remains plenty for you to do by crowning the edifice, in extending improvements over our vast, as yet unconquered regions, larger in extent than some European kingdoms.'[64] The humanitarian rhetoric of regret that informs Bull's reconstruction of frontier conflict is finally subsumed by a more celebratory mythology of foundation, a characteristic of reflections on the early years that prevailed into the twentieth century and beyond.

RECALLING THE
ELLISTON INCIDENT

∎

In 1992 the artist Siv Grava supervised members of the Elliston community in a search for images to represent the district's life and culture
on the walls of both the Community Agricultural Hall and the public
conveniences on the foreshore, producing one of South Australia's
biggest and most distinctive murals. The community found historical,
agricultural, fishing and sporting images to celebrate this west coast
country town's sense of what matters. On the north-western side of the
building, around the back, is a representation of an Indigenous family
standing on a cliff top staring out at the sun setting on Waterloo Bay.
At their feet are shells, suggesting the dozens of middens and campsites
that still can be found along the coast. The image hints at a number
of narratives. Only a small percentage of the wall space of the building
is given over to representations of Indigenous experience. The family
stands on a cliff edge at sunset, the prosaic nineteenth-century trope
encouraging the viewer to accept the idea that the Aborigines have had
their day. By 1992, the image suggests, the traces in this country of
the Nauo, the Wirangu and the Kukutha are as fragile and transitory
as the middens they have left behind. They belong to a *pre*-history, they
survive only as fragile archaeological evidence in the shifting sands.

The image of Aboriginal people on a cliff edge hints at popular
memories of a series of events in the history of the Elliston district.
There still circulates on the west coast (and beyond) shadowy, incom-
plete fragments of a local legend about Indigenous people driven to
their deaths over a cliff near Elliston as payback for the murders of two
or three settlers.

Typical of the *written* versions of the Elliston incident is 'The
Massacre that Mangultie Did Not Forget' by Betty Mac, published in

Mural on Community Agricultural Hall at Elliston
(photograph by Rick Hosking)

Detail of the mural on the Community Agricultural Hall at
Elliston (photograph by Rick Hosking)

the *Mail* of 30 April 1932 and containing many of the details that have circulated since the late nineteenth century. A hut at Lake Newland is the scene, a shepherd and his two sons described. The shepherd is murdered by an Indigenous man named Mangultie. When the sons return to the hut 'ready and hungry for their "tea" . . . Mangultie, an exultant gleam in his eye, pointed towards the camp oven. "Tea in there!" he said.'[1] The sons find their father's head roasting in the camp oven, his body later discovered some distance away from the hut. The police arrive and an unnamed 'trooper' takes charge, a man 'who folk to this day say could strike terror into the heart of any erring blackfellow by his appearance and demeanour'. Horsemen assemble with their dogs and round up the Indigenous people of the district and drive them over the cliffs.[2]

Another substantial representation of the story is local author Neil Thompson's 1969 novel *The Elliston Incident*,[3] which details a dark and violent story of the rising of the Wirangi [sic] and Kukutha people, led by their 'Chief' Jaggal, against the white settlers of the west coast some time last century. The discovery of the body of a decapitated shepherd named John Hamp, his head found roasting in a camp oven, provokes the whites to retaliate against the Aborigines for the murder. A band of vigilante horsemen is organised, a huge policeman named Gehirty [sic] taking a leading role; the Wirangi are rounded up and driven over the cliffs (here named 'the Bluffs') to the south of Elliston. The novel describes 20 deaths.

As a journalist observed in 1935, no 'episode in connection with the aborigines in South Australia has raised more controversy than the "massacre" of Waterloo Bay, somewhere about 1848'.[4] Since at least the 1850s there has been community debate about whether the massacre actually took place, a debate that reveals a great deal about uneasy memories of our pioneer past and of violence on the frontier. Every decade or so another version of the Elliston 'incident' is published, the details disputed, letters written to the editor, the only certainty that of contestation and disagreement.

Is there *any* historical basis for this gothic tale? Most versions of the story begin with the murder of the hutkeeper John Hamp.[5] He was killed near Weepra Spring on 23 June 1848, on William Pinkerton's[6] Stony Point station near Lake Newland. His body was found some distance from his hut, and it appears that when attacked he had been walking towards the scrub with a cross-cut saw to cut timber for fuel.

He had left his firearms behind in the hut. A number of spear wounds and a deep laceration to the left side of his head were described as having caused his death. Hamp is buried near the site of the hut at Weepra Spring, the site marked today by a plain granite memorial.

Hamp's death was followed in August 1848 by an 'affray', the shooting of at least one Aborigine by William Pinkerton's overseer, George Stewart, at Lake Newland after the theft of a shirt from the hut of a shepherd, John Wood.[7] The victim is not named in any official account. Lance-Corporal James Geharty's report[8] records that the victim was shot through the stomach: when Geharty went to the site a month after the shooting, the body had been mostly eaten by dingoes. No action was taken against Stewart and Wood.

In May 1849 the deaths of five 'natives' were reported: Karakundere[9] and Yurdlarir (boys of ten or thirteen), Puyultu and Ngamania (husband and wife), and Pirrapa (an infant), all of whom had eaten arsenic-poisoned flour stolen by an Aboriginal youth called Illeri from a hut on William R. Mortlock's station near Yeelanna. The person responsible was the hut-keeper, Patrick Dwyer, who was later arrested by Inspector Alexander Tolmer, charged with murder but then released by Charles J. Driver, the Government Resident in Port Lincoln.[10] Dwyer left South Australia shortly after for the United States. This episode may be the source of a number of local legends about similar poisonings elsewhere in the colony[11] and may have precipitated the payback murder of Captain James Rigby Beevor on 3 May 1849 and that of Anne Easton on 7 May 1849.

Captain Beevor[12] was in partnership with E.B. Lodwick on Tornto (also spelled Taunto and Tonto), about 80 kilometres north-west of Port Lincoln, between Mount Hope and Warrow. On the morning of 3 May, Lodwick had gone off to look after the sheep, leaving Beevor with three Indigenous men, one woman and a child, Beevor's servant, the latter having been sent out that morning to recover a tether rope and a horse. That evening Lodwick returned to find Beevor lying outside the hut with two spears through his heart, the hut ransacked and £70 value of goods taken. Beevor had been making a chair outside his hut when attacked by what seemed to have been a number of Indigenous people, including his young servant.[13] Beevor is buried in the Happy Valley cemetery near Port Lincoln.[14]

Anne (or Annie) Easton[15] was the first white woman to take up residence in the Lake Hamilton district which had only been settled for about a year. Her husband James was employed on Edward Bowyer Vaux's Lake Hamilton Run, the neighbouring lease to Beevor's.[16] After her murder, James Easton gave evidence that he had left his wife, who was still in bed, with the instruction that she should employ 'a native and his wife' to cut grass 'for the purpose of putting into a bed-tick'.[17] When he returned, he found the grass cut outside the hut door and, inside, his wife's body speared in several places 'on the bed-place' on the floor. Some commentators suggested that she was raped,[18] but Geharty's evidence asserted she died from the effects of a number of wounds: three to her breast, another through both cheeks, one in the back of her neck and a heavy bruise on her thigh.[19] The hut had been rifled, and one of the items stolen, the ramrod of a gun, would later be found in the possession of suspects.[20] Her infant six-week-old son Alfred (whom she was apparently dressing when she was attacked) was unharmed. When discovered, the naked child was exhausted from crying all day beside his dead mother.[21] Easton is buried in what is now the Lake Hamilton cemetery. The two men convicted and hanged for her murder are buried in the grounds of the old Port Lincoln police station.

The next 'affray' occurred three weeks after Easton's death, on 27 May 1849, on Thomas Cooper Horn's[22] Kappawanta Run, which

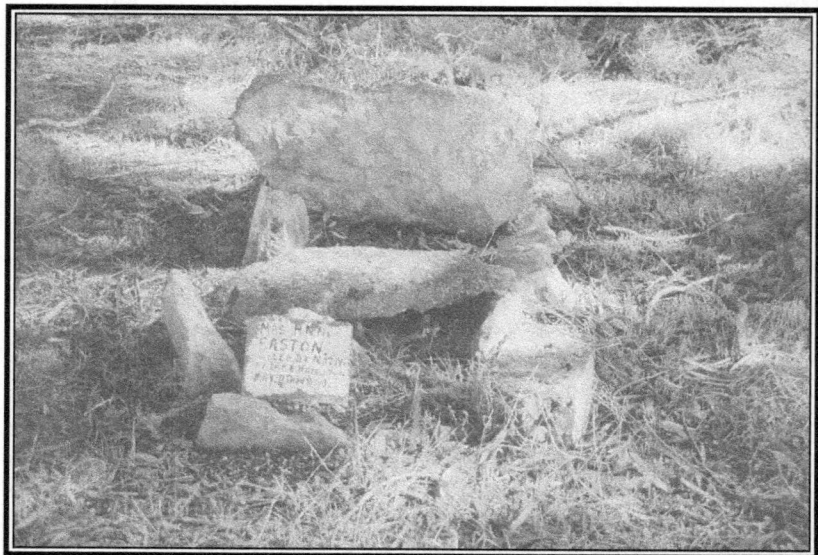

Annie Easton's grave (photograph by Rick Hosking)

centred on Bramfield and extended as far west as Waterloo Bay.[23] Stores were taken from a hut and hutkeeper David Allen and shepherd James Brown threatened. Horn and some of his station hands gave chase, and when they came up on the fleeing party, spears were thrown and shots fired. The suspects then split into two, Horn and his men following one group to the Waterloo Bay cliffs, which the suspects climbed down attempting to escape. Horn and his men fired on them: two were killed on the spot and one died of wounds later. Five other Aboriginal people were apprehended in possession of stolen goods.

Government Resident Charles J. Driver and Tolmer both have recorded detailed accounts of the 'affray'. Driver notes that Horn and some of his employees pursued the Aborigines to the cliffs, and after a brief conflict two were killed and eight captured.[24] Tolmer reports the same episode and similarly does not mention large numbers of casualties,[25] describing his arrival at Horn's station and the subsequent pursuit which resulted in several arrests.[26]

The colonial criminal justice system took its full course with those arrested and charged over the various offences, the authorities taking considerable care to demonstrate that British justice would prevail. In September 1849 Neulatta (or Neentulta or Needgalta), Keelgulta (or Kulyulta, Kulgulta or Culgalta), Pulluruninga and Yabmanna were escorted back to Adelaide. Needgalta and Kulgulta (an old man) were tried and convicted of Beevor's murder and sentenced to death.[27] They were returned from Adelaide to Taunto, and hanged from a red gum on a spring cart scaffold outside Beevor's hut.[28] Father and son Ngálta (Ilgalti) and Bakkilti (or Pakilte, and sometimes spelled Bakilta) and Pularpintye (or Purtapintye) were charged with the murder of Easton, but both were acquitted for lack of evidence.[29] Korlo was also charged with being an accessory before the fact of the murder of Easton. Yaingulta, Wirao, Winulla and Yaluma were arrested and charged with various offences for the attack on Horn's station.

Mingulta and Malgalta were arrested a little later in Port Lincoln by Trooper Geharty and charged with the murder over a year before of John Hamp.[30] They were found guilty and sentenced to death but later released when doubts were raised about the value of 'native testimony' collected by Geharty – such testimony in other cases against white men had been ruled insufficient to warrant a conviction.[31] Before their release they were taken back to Taunto to witness the hangings of Neentulta and Keelgulta.[32]

There were more arrests in the months to come. One of the most poignant of the stories that has survived is that of Maltalta, who was arrested by Geharty in February 1850, and charged as an accomplice in Hamp's murder. Maltalta (or Multulti) was sent to Adelaide but only remained in Adelaide Gaol a few days, released in Adelaide for lack of evidence.[33] He tried to walk home to his country but was intercepted by a group of Narrunga men from Yorke Peninsula and executed as a trespasser. During the murder trial Kanyana, a boy of 12 years of age, gave evidence that when Maltalta first arrived in their camp he had said his name was Maltalta and that 'he was going around to his country', that is, walking home. The four men charged with his murder were found guilty and sentenced to be hanged on 9 June 1851. The court was well aware that two legal systems had come into violent and intractable conflict but was determined that British criminal justice would prevail.[34]

Was there a massacre? There seems to be no *direct* evidence of any 'crusade against the natives' in the official documents from the period 1848–1850. The outletter book kept by Charles Driver still exists, but there is no description of a massacre to be found in any of the many letters Driver sent to the colonial secretary's office in the period in question.[35] There is only one letter that might be read as suggesting that there was a group of vigilantes out searching for the alleged murderers.

Similarly there is no *direct* evidence in the memoirs written by individuals who were directly involved in the events of 1848–1849. None of the policemen involved (Geharty, Tolmer and Henry Holroyd) has anything to say about a massacre on the scale described in the legend. Nathaniel Hailes, Charles Driver's clerk, does not report any such event in his memoirs. Nor has Sub-Protector (and later Court Translator) Pastor Clamor Schürmann anything to say.[36]

Nevertheless, it seems that an aggregation of details drawn from a number of these episodes from 1848 and 1849 is responsible for the more dramatic late-nineteenth and early-twentieth century versions of the 'Elliston incident'. The pillaging of Horn's hut, the subsequent pursuit by Horn and his men, some shooting and deaths on the cliffs overlooking Waterloo Bay: these details can be seen as the origins of many of the details that will later become integral to the legend.

Whatever did (or did not) happen in and around Elliston in the late 1840s has been argued about for a long time, at least since the first version of the story was published. 'H.J.C's 'A Reminiscence of Port

Lincoln' appeared on Saturday 14 August 1880 in the *Adelaide Observer*. This piece, which has been taken as 'history' by some commentators, was in fact published in 'The Miscellany' section of the *Observer*, subtitled 'Literature'.[37] H.J.C. are the initials of Henry John Congreve (1829–1918), the brother of the writer 'Maud Jean Franc'. Congreve arrived in South Australia in 1849 on the *Trafalgar*, and worked variously as a doctor, bullock driver and newspaper editor. He lived for 18 months in Port Lincoln on various pastoral runs, later moving to Burra, then Gawler. He left South Australia for the Victorian diggings in 1851 and did not return to South Australia until 1880.[38] Congreve published many short stories in newspapers and magazines in South Australia and other colonies. He was interested in writing *creatively* about the sensational, gothic aspects of frontier and bush experience: murders, massacres, lost children, lonely graves and so on. Such popular and ephemeral pieces filled the literary pages of most Australian newspapers of the period.[39]

Congreve's version of the Elliston incident contains many of the controversial details that later appear in the more colourful versions (published or otherwise) of what *might* have happened. It is a fanciful and sometimes wildly inaccurate fictionalising of the events of the late 1840s. In lurid fashion, the piece describes four murders by an Aborigine called Multulti (the name of one of the suspects in the Hamp murder arrested by Geharty in 1849). Multulti, it is claimed, 'was motivated by a desire to expel the whites from the country'. The first murder is that of Captain B – while the latter was engaged in carpentry. The second, of Mary, the 'young and pretty wife' of a shepherd and the object of Multulti's 'fierce wishes', and the third, of Mary's baby son. The fourth, of an *unnamed* hutkeeper, who was surprised while cutting wood and killed when his head was cut in half with his crosscut saw 'while yet alive'. The piece includes some of what will become the characteristic features of the legend: the murders themselves, one committed with a cross-cut saw; a retaliatory 'drive' organised by Harry, the victim Mary's husband; the shooting of many Aboriginal people, the survivors driven over a cliff; the capture of Mary's killers and their later execution outside Captain B – 's hut. Multulti survived, was captured much later and died in Adelaide. Interestingly, Congreve does *not* refer to a head in a camp oven, nor does he call the hutkeeper Hamp.

Congreve's representation of Multulti includes the suggestion that 'from an accident in childhood he had been crippled in one foot'[40] so that, once the pursuit started, the settlers were able to track him and his party to their camp. Sergeant Geharty's evidence at the trial of Mingulta and Malgalta (the two accused of Hamp's murder) reveals that at least part of the prosecution's case against Mingalta was based on his having an injured great toe, which enabled his footprints to be tracked by Police-Constable John Dann for 20 miles.[41]

Who might have been 'Mr S – ,' the 'captain' of the vigilante posse? When the nineteenth-century novelist employs the convention of using only the initial letter of a surname, it can be taken to mean that that character is based on a real individual and the writer is preserving his true identity. Congreve may have had in mind George Stewart, William Pinkerton's overseer and a man implicated in a number of 'unhappy collisions'. Congreve worked on a number of different runs in the Port Lincoln district between 1849 and 1851 and, given the relatively small number of settlers on the coast at that time, it is likely that he knew Stewart and thus may have heard of his involvement in collisions with Aboriginal people.[42]

Within a fortnight of its publication, Congreve's short story attracted comment. G.K., a west coast resident, wrote to the *Observer* to point out 'errors' in Congreve's piece, insisting: that the child survived (and still lives, says 'G.K.'); that Congreve's account of the fight was 'highly coloured'; that only one Aboriginal man was shot dead and none of the settlers was injured; that 'the man Hemp [*sic*] who had his head sawn open, was murdered some time previously'; and that 'Harry' the husband of the murdered women was 'as sane of mind as H.J.C. himself, and perhaps possessing a better memory'.[43] The *Observer* asked Congreve to respond to these accusations. In an 'explanation' printed beneath G.K.'s letter, Congreve makes several points: he had written from memory; he had lived at the very hut where the executions had occurred (at Taunto); he had been a member of a party sent out to capture Multulti, a 'Lachlan blackfellow'; and he was pleased to discover the child had lived. Congreve added this rider:

> I never intended my sketch to have the weight of an historical document. It was merely written as illustrative of the trials and dangers of the early settlers . . . It would not be wise (if able) to more fully particularize localities or individuals concerned in black encounters, as it might lead to unpleasant interference from those who are concerned with the protection of the aborigines.[44]

Congreve insists his 'sketch' is not history but fiction designed to 'illustrate'. But as G.K. demonstrates and Congreve admits, the sketch exaggerates and distorts what (probably) happened. Congreve's piece contributes to the developing national myth of the violent, blood-thirsty, vengeful 'black' and the dark unholy fight on the frontier that, like drought, floods and fire, had to be fought and won by the pioneer before the 'new heaven and new earth' might be achieved.[45] Congreve also admits that covert and unreported violence did occur in 'black encounters'.

The second published reference to the 'Waterloo Bay Massacre' is an oblique reference in a short story called 'Doctor' by Ellen Liston, published in the *Observer* of 17 June 1882. Rick Hosking has argued else-where[46] that Liston must have read Congreve's 'A Reminiscence of Port Lincoln', in that in the same issue (14 August 1880) in which Congreve's piece appeared, Liston published a poem 'The Fire King: A Reminiscence of 1851'.[47] She probably heard the story of Annie Easton's death when she worked as a governess on Nilkerloo Station between 1869 and 1872 – her employer just happened to be John Chipp Hamp, the son of the John Hamp who was murdered at Weepra Spring in 1848.

The incident at the centre of Liston's short story 'Doctor' seems to be based loosely on the historical murder of the shepherd's wife Anne Easton at Lake Hamilton. In the Liston story, Kit, the pregnant wife of a shepherd, is attacked by an Aboriginal man called Coomultie, but she does not die; her life is saved by a dog called Doctor who kills Coomultie. As a consequence of the attack, Kit loses her baby, pro-voking what Liston calls 'a crusade against the natives' organised by the 'hands' – that is, employees from the surrounding stations, not lease-holders nor police.[48]

Did Liston hear whispers about a massacre while she worked on Nilkerloo? Perhaps John Chipp Hamp told her the story – he seems to have told just about everyone else. If a massacre did occur, were the 'hands' responsible? There is some evidence that while official parties led by Tolmer and Geharty were out and about in the field in search of those responsible for the killings, there were also unofficial parties in the field. Historian Greg Charter notes that on 16 May 1849, John Stewart Brown, Charles Driver's clerk in Port Lincoln, reported to the colonial secretary's office that 'there were three separate parties of volunteers out at that time'. Charter suggests that this information is consistent with the major component of the later stories, i.e. a party of armed horsemen in pursuit of a large body of Aborigines in the vicinity of Elliston near the end of the decade and indicates that if the massacre took place it occurred following the Beevor and Easton murders.'[49]

Another interesting detail about the publication history of Liston's short story 'Doctor' emerges from the fact that it was reprinted twice in 1936 – the centenary of European settlement in South Australia. A revised version of 'Doctor' (with significant editorial changes) appeared in a volume celebrating women's roles in European settlement, the anthology *A Book of South Australia: Women in the First Hundred Years*.[50] It was then reprinted (in its original 1882 *Observer* version) in *Pioneers: Stories by Ellen Liston*. The editors of the revised version removed three paragraphs from the original. The first contains a reference to 'troublesome' blacks. The second has Liston's description of a 'vast and terrible stillness' that pressed so heavily upon her character that she was 'tempted to flee away shrieking as from some unholy presence'. The third paragraph mentions the 'muster of hands from several stations . . . who had gone in for a crusade against the natives'. The removal of these paragraphs may have had something to do with the kinds of memories of pioneering the editors wished to valorise in 1936, South Australia's Centennial Year. Better erase from the record any suggestion of settlers' violence against Aborigines, any unease about colonial history. Liston's character Kit's sensing of an 'unholy presence' in this frontier landscape can be read these days as the discovery of the reality of Indigenous presence, even if that presence is demonised, represented in crudely Manichean terms. Liston's phrase reveals what cultural historian J.J. Healy has described as 'the great rich . . . unease' evident in much nineteenth-century Australian writing,[51] the melancholy strain which reveals the dark side of the Australian Dream.[52]

By the turn of the century a well-developed local legend was circulating about the 'Elliston incident', a story that became part of the folklore of South Australia: one of the 1926 correspondents to the *Register* who claimed he first heard the story in 1869 or 1870.[53] However, the earliest reference to the *legend* of the Elliston massacre – that is, to the fact of a oral account circulating on the west coast, and a mocking description of the circumstances under which it might be retold – first appeared in the *Register* and was then later reprinted in a 1906 travel book called *The Real West Coast: A New Picture of a Rumour-Damaged Country* by E.W. Parish. Parish claimed that while travelling around the coast with a friend he had heard 'the tragic legend' told a dozen or more times, the details of which 'varied according to the degree of elasticity of the narrator's veracity'. Parish records, in what he calls a 'literary tabloid', most of the familiar details: the son discovering his murdered father's head in a camp oven; the rounding up of the supposed Aboriginal murderers by a posse of horsemen; the 'herding' over the Elliston cliffs and significant numbers of casualties.[54] Parish's scornful response to the storytellers who pressed themselves on him may seem callous and insensitive, but nevertheless his understanding of the social functions of local legends is apparent. Parish also records how he and his companion were told the story so often that they were forced to develop a strategy to deflect yet more retellings. The west coast seems to have been peopled with yarnspinners keen to claim their right as locals to tell the story.

Former policeman Thomas Clode probably knew some of the same informants who had earbashed Parish. Clode joined the South Australian police force in 1865, served for many years on the west coast and for some time was stationed at Venus Bay. In 1915 his recollections were published in the *Register*, including what should now be seen as many of the conventional details: Hamp's murder, his son discovering the head in the camp oven, a posse of constables under Sergeant Geraghty [*sic*] who rounded up the blacks and drove them over the cliffs. Clode's version contains two new details: he insists that John Chipp Hamp ran away after finding his father's head in the oven, but 'the blacks traced him, and kept him for three months before the police found him'.[55] This is the only version of the 'Elliston Incident' which gestures towards the 'captivity narrative' tradition.

In 1926 an innocent letter from John Dow to the editor of the *Register*, inquiring how Waterloo Bay got its name, made the question of the 'massacre' a matter of public debate.[56] West coaster Archie Beviss responded three weeks later, provoking a ding-dong battle between *Register* journalist A.T. Saunders and Beviss in the pages of the paper. At issue was the authenticity of the Elliston legend, Beviss relying on hearsay evidence recounted in yarns, Saunders on what he could establish on the official record. The battle was joined by correspondents from both sides of the debate, from all around South Australia and from Elliston residents in particular.

Beviss's name is now associated forever with the most bloodthirsty of the versions of the legend. He claims to have heard about the massacre from, among others, 'the late Mr John Chip [*sic*] Hamp and Sgt. Garretty [*sic*]', both of whom he names as 'principals'. He records the main features of the story as follows. Hamp (then 16 years old and a shepherd) finds his father's head in a camp oven, the head cut off with a crosscut saw. While the sergeant is investigating, a second murder of a woman occurs, prompting 'Garretty' to approach the government demanding drastic action. The government, Beviss insists, 'granted the request, and the sergeant organised a force 160 strong, and planned the drive', which resulted in about 260 Aboriginal people being driven over the Elliston cliffs. The account ends as follows:

> The effect of the drive was tranquillity among the blacks from Port
> Lincoln to Fowler's Bay. To use Sgt. Garratty's [*sic*] words, as he
> told me over 40 years ago, 'Show them a gun or crack a whip, and
> it is quite sufficient.' His last words were, 'I had a good lot of men
> with me then. I would not like to try it now.' The sergeant named
> the place Waterloo Bay after what he saw happened.[57]

Many of Beviss's assertions can be challenged. Geharty did not name Waterloo Bay.[58] The husband of the murdered woman Ann Easton could not have been 'well in the van of the drive'; James Easton went to Adelaide after his wife's murder and it seems he never returned to the west coast. Their son Alfred was raised by the pastoralist Andrew Tennant.[59] There is no evidence that the government sanctioned any 'drive'. Finally, if the vigilante party contained 160 men, given what happened after the Rufus incident near Lake Victoria when a number of participants recorded their recollections, it is likely that at least one or two manuscript accounts of the massacre would have survived. No such diary or journal accounts exist.

In spite of many inaccuracies, the influence of the Beviss version of the story was strong enough to shape many later descriptions of the district and its lurid history. A typical note is struck in P. Hosking's 1936 assertion that Elliston is located on Waterloo Bay, the latter 'appropriately named on account of the sad stories, so numerous in this part of the State, of the outrages by aboriginals and reprisals by white settlers'.[60]

Similarly J.F. O'Dea's 1960s pamphlet held in the Mortlock Library notes that 'it is generally agreed that the story is basicly [*sic*] correct although generally not accepted by Historians due to lack of documented evidence'.[61] O'Dea notes that 'one elderly man who was spoken to some years ago and whose father was said to be in the 'drive' told me that the infamous Trooper Geharty told those who took part that "it was a terrible thing that they had done and there would be no record made of the incident"'.[62]

Many versions of the story in print claim to rely on hearsay evidence from individuals either living in the Elliston district at the time of the alleged massacre, or from the relatives of witnesses. When the claim to authority is based on 'sources' living in or around the Elliston district, such versions reveal one of the typical characteristics of local legends: that local identities play a key role in fixing one version of the truth. John Chipp Hamp (John Hamp's son) and Sergeant James Geharty are often mentioned as telling the story of the incident, for many years after the event. Numbers of commentators quote one or the other or even both. But it is unlikely that John Chipp Hamp should have been (as Beviss insists) one of the principals in any massacre: his obituary in the *Observer* notes that he was 12 when his father was murdered.[63]

Yet it does seem that John Chipp Hamp was partly responsible for spreading the legend of his father's death. D.R. Myers lived on Oaklands, the neighbouring property to Chickerloo which John Chipp Hamp took over in 1865. As an old man of 85, Myers reports in a reminiscence in the *Port Lincoln Times* in 1931 that:

> Many a time I have heard my old friend and neighbour [John Hamp] . . . tell of that tragedy, and I have seen his father's grave. . . . Such a grim and dreadful happening caused great wrath and indignation among the white folk in this isolated part of the State. Police and settlers scoured the country on horseback, collected many of the natives and drove them towards Waterloo Bay, frightening them thoroughly. Nowadays, this drive is known as the Waterloo Bay massacre, and the results have been exaggerated, the early settlers being loath to speak of it.[64]

While travelling with John Chipp Hamp, N.A. Richardson also heard him tell the story. Writing in the *Register* in 1931, he describes how:

> Mr Hamp told us the story of his discovering his father murdered by the natives; the head had been cut off the body, and was in the camp oven in the fireplace. He told me of the rally made by

the few settlers then in the district, and of how they rounded up the natives, and how they made for the coast, where many of them were driven over the rocks, and perished in the sea. He said that was how the place became known as Waterloo Bay. The real murderer was afterwards arrested and hanged close to where Mr Hamp sen., was killed. Was it likely that those few settlers were going to report their escapade to the police – the nearest of whom were then stationed at Port Lincoln, some 120 miles away?[65]

And as late as 1970, writing in the *Advertiser*, the writer Max Fatchen quotes Arthur Betteridge-MacBeth who met the 70-year-old Hamp northwest of Port Augusta around the turn of the century:

he told me . . . about a massacre of aborigines after the death of his father. . . . he told me how he and his elder brother as boys had returned from herding sheep and had found their father's head in a camp oven. Hamp had said that a chain of men had been formed and they ranged across the countryside driving the aborigines to the coast and over the cliff into the sea. He never named the cliff.[66]

Within the Hamp family opinion is divided about their ancestor's powers of recall. To begin with, Fatchen quotes Rupert Giles, a great-grandson of John Hamp:

The story handed down by Mr Giles's father and his cousins was that John Hamp's head was found in the oven by his son. The cousins' version was that the settlers were so incensed that they rallied together, mustered all the aborigines in the vicinity and drove them into the sea.[67]

But at least one member of the Hamp family did not believe his grandfather's yarn. Dr Edward J[ohn?] C[hipp?] Hamp wrote to the *Advertiser* in 1937 with the view that:

Mr J.D. Somerville['s] exceptionally careful research work . . . shows conclusively that the alleged massacre never occurred, and that the head in the camp oven story is a myth. . . . [T]he early settlers did not take the law into their own hands, as is commonly depicted'.[68]

Many years later, in a letter to P.J. Baillie, Dr Hamp continued to pour scorn on the Beviss version of the story:

[t]here would never have been this interest in the Hamp family, had it not been for the murder and the story of the head in the oven, which was invented by the late drover, Archie Bevis [*sic*], who was a self-confessed liar. The press publish references and the stories become resurrected. Descendants of the old pioneers believe the Bevis story, and because of this, the only proof positive (in spite of the findings at the Coroner's Inquest and the trial of the natives Mingalta and Malgalta), is to view the skeleton, because there are still plenty of people who believe that the Police of those days deliberately suppressed the truth, and dreadfully untrue indictment, linked up with the alleged massacre of natives at Waterloo Bay, where they were said to have been driven over the cliffs to certain death. This too is a lie.[69]

No doubt Hamp's grandson is right: an autopsy *might* settle the matter.

There are problems with all these versions. Hamp's son John Chipp Hamp is *not* mentioned as being present as a shepherd on Pinkerton's Stoney Point Run in any *Register* account of the later trial, nor in any of the letters to the colonial secretary's office from Charles Driver,[70] nor by Police Commissioner George Dashwood in his quarterly returns which mention the murder.[71] The only named companion for whom Hamp worked as hutkeeper was Henry Hammond, the man who found the body and reported the murder to the overseer, George Stewart.[72] The son John Chipp Hamp seems not even to have been present. Surely the poignancy of the detail of a son discovering his father's murdered body would have attracted at least one of those individuals close to the events to have recorded the fact of his presence. So why did John Chipp Hamp tell the story that he had discovered his father's body, not once but many times? Did *he* invent the detail about the head in the camp oven? Or did he accept at face value a yarn circulated by others such as Beviss?

James Geharty's role in the alleged affair is equally problematic. He is an individual about whom numbers of yarns have circulated. He seems to have led the kind of life on the west coast for which William Willshire (a colleague in the South Australian Police Force) would later become notorious in the Northern Territory. Geharty's superior officer, Henry Holroyd, describes him as possessing a 'grand dash of military style which was very effective among wild natives and rough bushmen' and also notes that there 'was an extraordinary facet in the native character which was invaluable to us [policemen]. . . . They had a great fear of the police and on the occasions of lawbreaking they gave us every assistance in finding the culprits.[73] One suspects that Geharty may have had something to do with polishing that facet of the native character. He was once quoted as saying that 'the blacks' were easily managed – 'show them a gun or crack a whip and it is quite sufficient'.[74] In 1849 writer and local historian Neil Thompson repeated[75] the oft-told story that Geharty often refused to gaol Aboriginal suspects and instead tied them to the wheels of his wagon to punish them. In *The Streaky Bay: A History of the Streaky Bay District* Thompson quotes Mr Roche, the husband of Geharty's grand-daughter: 'he was a big man and ran things his way. He'd go into a camp – "wagon-wheel" them – to make his point. He was hard, all right'.[76]

Hardly surprisingly, in 1849 there was some unease[77] expressed in the executive council about Geharty's methods in extracting confessions from the Hamp murder suspects. Their validity was questioned after the Bishop of Adelaide (among others) had presented a memorial to the council presenting reasons why the sentences of death should not be carried out.[78]

Numbers of commentators refer to Geharty's role as yarnspinner, usually citing him as an authority, an eyewitness, a participant, someone who *knew*. Robert Hull, of Elliston, wrote to the *Observer* in 1926 asserting that when he

> came to Colton in 1877, Sgt. Geharaty [*sic*] stayed with me often, and he told me a few things about the murders of blacks. He said they drove a mob over the cliffs near Waterloo Bay, but he did not say how many. I think the story is something like the snowball – the older it gets the bigger it grows. There is no doubt there was a drive. The place was along the cliffs south of the bay. The point or cape your correspondents speak about is called Cape Finniss.[79]

Another version of the same story was told in the *Advertiser* in 1932 by M.S.W. Kenny, also a native of Colton:

> There was nothing in this yarn . . . I lived 50 years behind the bar [of the Colton Hotel] and heard most things. I have the true story first hand from Sergeant O'Garaghty [*sic*], a very fine type of wild Irishman who had left the police force. . . . He said that the blacks had been bad . . . and that about 200 bushmen on horseback drove

the blacks north. One lubra may have fallen over the cliffs, but the wholesale massacre is all moonshine.[80]

These last two versions seem to capture some of the details about what happened at Horn's Bramfield Run in May 1849, although the numbers involved seem to have grown somewhat with the various retellings of the story. As Neil Thompson notes, if as many as 200 bushmen were involved, 'no secret of that dimension could possibly have been kept'.[81] Some of these versions of the story (perhaps collected from Geharty) will typically dismiss reports of a 'massacre' as either a 'legend', a 'yarn', a 'snowball' or 'moonshine', They include details of a settlers' muster or drive of an indeterminate number of Aboriginal people and a cliff-top setting, but usually it is insisted that there were either no casualties or perhaps only one or two.

The most macabre detail of the Elliston legend is that of the head in the camp oven. What does the historical record have to say? There is *no* evidence of Hamp's decapitation in any of the accounts by Charles Driver, nor in any police evidence given at the inquest, nor in the later trial of Mingulta and Malgalta for Hamp's murder. Driver reported to the colonial secretary that 'the deceased had apparently been waddied to death, and his skull sawn nearly half round with a hand-saw'.[82] Police Commissioner Dashwood, quoting reports from Geharty, notes that 'the murder has been attended with peculiar barbarity, the skull having been divided with a handsaw'.[83] Dashwood's quarterly report ending 30 June 1848 does, however, give a slightly different version. The murder is described as being

> of a most barbarous character, the perpetrators of this horrid deed having sawed their victim's head into two pieces with a hand saw which was found in the hut, with blood and hair adhering to it.[84]

The *Register* account of the trial does not mention Hamp's decapitation. The details of his fatal injuries can be found in evidence given by Pinkerton's overseer, George Stewart, a witness in the murder trial in the Supreme Court in Adelaide in September 1849. Stewart and two police constables had found Hamp's body on 23 June 1848. Stewart insisted that Hamp's:

> head was cut all over as if he had been beaten with sticks. There was one very deep wound near the left ear. It appeared to have

been done by a saw. There was a hole in his trowsers as if occasioned by a spear. His hands were also wounded.[85]

Stewart also found a bloodstained spear between the hut and where Hamp's body had been found, and footprints which he recognised as belonging to one of the suspects, Mingulta, whose 'great toe' was deformed. Stewart identified a saw as the property of Mr Pinkerton. 'It was found inside the hut with blood and grey hair upon it. Hamp's hair was grey, and his brains were visible through the wound made with the saw in his head'.[86]

Extensive notes were taken by Judge Charles Cooper from the evidence presented by the police during the trial of Hamp's alleged murderers. That evidence was later used to bring doubt on the guilt of Mingulta and Malgalta and eventually to save them from the gallows.[87] Cooper records the statement given by the 'native aboriginal witness' Ninnulta as follows:

> This witness stated that he knew Tommy; – that the Prisoners – Mingulta and Malgalta and others speared him; – that he died by spears; – that Malgalta threw the first spear; – Mingulta threw the next; – that Monalta and others speared him; – that he was speared on the side; – that Korti Warrie is the name of the place; – that there is water near it; permanent water; – that he knew a saw produced [as evidence in court]; – that a man sawed the head with it; – that he [Ninnulta] was there; – that the Prisoners were there; – that the saw was put outside a hut; – that the prisoners went to the sands where the scrub was; – that there is water in the sands; – that they went to Willi Narri; – that Korti Warri[88] is a lake place; – that the Prisoners cut the lake; went over it; – that witness knew Tommy[89] a long time ago, and so did the Prisoner Mingulta; – that Tommy was his only name; – that when the men went away Tommy was lying in the plain in the grass; – that all the men who were there speared him; – there was one (wound) on his breast and another there also; Normulta threw the spear; – that the Prisoners were there and they speared also.[90]

Aside from its intrinsic interest, the evidence of Ninnulta clearly establishes that it was the *spearing* of Hamp that most interested the prosecution, not the wounds to his head. It appears that the prosecution also pursued this same line of argument with later witnesses. George

Stewart and Police Constable Dann both mention Hamp's head wound. Both saw the body and later gave evidence in the Supreme Court. First, Stewart's evidence, which clearly indicates that Hamp's head was still on his shoulders:

> on the 24rd of that month [June 1848] his [Hamp's] dead body was found, lying with the face partly down; – that the head was cut all over, as if struck with sticks; – and there was a deep wound over the left ear, which appeared to have been done with a sharp instrument; – that there was a mark like a spear mark, and a hole in his trowsers; – that the body was not examined; it was much mutilated, and all covered over with blood; – the head and the hands were much mutilated . . .

The witness was then shown the saw which was presented as evidence.

> It belongs to Mr Pinkerton. I saw it in Hamp's hut; – it was found inside the hut; – there were marks of blood and hair on it; – grey hair: Hamp had grey hair.[91]

Police Constable John Dann then gave his evidence:

> that he was in company with Stewart when the body was found; that there was blood on the head and the hands; – on the head there was a deep cut through the skull; – the brain was partly out; – the head and face and hands were battered about. Under the waistcoat there was a hole; – Witness did not see how deep it went.[92]

In spite of the crown's insistence during the trial in September 1849 that spear wounds killed Hamp, it seems that as early as July 1848 the story of his decapitation was beginning to circulate on the west coast. One early suggestion is in the *South Australian*'s account of the murder written by a local correspondent, which states that Hamp 'had no spear wound, but his head had been sawn down. The hand saw, which had evidently been the instrument of death, was lying near him'.[93] It may be that 'sawn down' means 'sawn off'. By 1882 the popular view seems to have been held that Hamp had been decapitated: a unequivocal reference to Hamp's head being 'cut off with a saw' is in Alexander Tolmer's *Reminiscences* published in that year.[94]

Whatever the truth, as early as 1851 the detail of Hamp's head wound had become synonymous with the barbarity of Aboriginal people.

In a letter by Charles Driver detailing the killing of the shepherd Crocker by Kumbilti, the following remarks were made about the nature of the violence committed by Aboriginal people against Europeans:

> their murders have always been committed in strong parties attended by wanton destruction of property, and with the barbarous mangling of the dead, such as sawing the head, or beating it to a pulp, or burying an axe in it . . . the late atrocities committed by the Natives in this district, are merely the natural working of an unformed system.[95]

While there may be no evidence that Hamp was decapitated, the head in the camp oven story has helped shape the memory of frontier violence in South Australia. It is illuminating, however, to compare the circumstances of Hamp's death with that of an Aboriginal man in the same district six years earlier. After the killings by Aborigines of a number of settlers in the Port Lincoln district in 1842, the government sent a detachment of soldiers into the field to track down the perpetrators. In early May there was a collision at Pillaworta station at the southern end of Arno Bay and an unknown number of Aboriginal people were killed. When the missionary Clamor Schürmann was called to identify the victims, he discovered that the soldiers had decapitated one of the bodies:

> The soldiers and the policemen stuck the head on a pole and put it on an old pig sty, forcing a short clay pipe between the teeth. I remonstrated with the Lieutenant [Hugonin] against the impropriety of such conduct but could not prevail upon him to put a stop to it.[96]

Perhaps the head in the camp oven detail evolved from the conflation of local memories of both the 1842 decapitation and the nature of Hamp's head wounds. Whatever the truth, the shocking nature of those wounds and the detail of the saw found in the hut was sufficiently colourful to precipitate a rumour that within fifty years was fully formed, and known by a whole community. In the absence of any scrutiny of the official record and of any detailed published memoirs from the period, the story quickly gathered momentum until thousands believed it.

Over time, the head in the camp oven story developed a life of its own, sometimes being told independently of any story associated with the Elliston district. Historian Jim Faull found one version when preparing his 1988 book *On the Edge*. In some cardboard boxes in the Ceduna Area School library are a number of memoirs of local people, some handwritten. One (by Murray Collins?) is titled 'The Pioneers' and contains this version of the 'head in the camp oven' story:

> Mr Hosking, another prominent pioneer – he later owned St Peters Island – built his homestead near Waranda Well. Years later, while alone in his hut, he was attacked and killed by blacks, who cut off his head and placed it in his camp oven.[97]

And what of that camp oven? There are *no* references to camp ovens in the prosecution evidence presented at the trial of Hamp's alleged murderers. There was, however, debate about a rather more prosaic 'pint pot . . . with WP [William Pinkerton engraved] on the bottom, and John Russell on the side' which was found in the possession of the accused Malgalta who was arrested by Police Corporal Geharty in Port Lincoln when he had arrived for the distribution of rations on the full moon. Under cross-examination Geharty admitted that Malgalta may have received the pot from another native. Mingulta was also arrested at that time on the evidence of his footprints.[98]

One intriguing detail about the head in the camp oven story is a letter from D.C. Amey, the District Clerk of the District Council of Streaky Bay, to P.J. Baillie, dated 1 April 1971 (note the date), in which it is asserted that 'Elliston couldn't claim the privilege of the historical site of the head in the camp oven incident – that the boy who made history in this connection was Baird [*sic*]'.[99] This remark refers to a notorious murder at Mount Hall in the Calca district in 1896 when Walter Richards was murdered by Joshua Beard (not Baird) who buried the body and then built a campfire over the grave on which he had cooked his food.[100] Amey suggests that storytellers describing the 'Elliston Massacre' yarn took the camp oven detail from stories about the murderer Beard circulating around the turn of the century. Amey may have been right, in that there are no references to the head in the camp oven published before the turn of the century.

The head in the camp oven story has since travelled far. It appears in a 1977 travel book about the Nullarbor, Basil Fuller's *Nullarbor Lifelines*. Travellers, it seems, are suckers for local legends – the locals have a field day when rubbernecks show up. Fuller was told that somewhere on Roe Plain:

is the grave of a young woman, Annie McGill, who died in
childbirth after the shock of seeing her husband lying dead, his
head in the oven. The unfortunate pioneer had been murdered
by Aborigines. Some say that the tribesmen had provocation for
this and other atrocities they committed, that there were occasions – after periods of constant stock spearing – when Aborigines
were rounded up by armed horsemen and driven over the ninety
metre high cliffs of the escarpment. However, when . . . I called
in Melbourne on Mr James Lawrence, senior Eucla telegraphist
before and after the turn of the century, though I listened to many
tales of the Roe Plain and the Hampton Tableland, there had been
no mention of happenings such as these. James Lawrence was not
a man to perpetuate such memories and perhaps he deliberately
suppressed them. The evidence of Anne's grave is inescapable.
However, it seems likely that the tales of the killings have been
exaggerated in the telling, and that exact recollection has faded
with the generations.[101]

Fuller's 'grim tale' preserves most of the salient features of the original
and offers some of the usual ways of interpreting the Elliston incident.
It demonstrates once more the uneasy equation of the pioneer's hardships with internecine skirmishing with Aborigines, the extermination
of whom is a necessary step in ensuring the pioneer's success. The yarn
notes that the Aborigines were provoked to violence. But as Fuller
remarks after James Lawrence failed to verify the yarn he had collected,
tales of the killings *might* have been exaggerated in the telling.

After 1926, most versions of the Elliston incident usually quote the
archival and newspaper record and notice that there is *no* evidence of
a massacre on the scale described by Congreve, Beviss or John Chipp
Hamp. The most rigorous attempts to examine the evidence for the
Elliston massacre are those of J.D. Somerville, A.T. Saunders, P.J. Baillie
and Greg Charter, all amateur or professional historians. After
examining the official records held in the South Australian Archives,
Somerville's view is that there is no *formal* evidence of a massacre, and
the 'affray' at Horn's station was the precipitating incident that helped
create the 'myth'.[102] P.J. Baillie worked with Somerville, and as his
unpublished research notes held in the Mortlock and his published
comments in the *Chronicle* make clear, he agreed with Somerville and
Saunders that 'this alleged massacre is based on the robbery of Thomas

Horne's hut (Horne's look-out) which was the subject of investigation by the Adelaide Supreme Court' and goes on to add that from this incident 'ambitious raconteurs have superimposed the massacre story, elevating modest fact to unbridled fancy'.[103] In his Flinders University honours thesis Greg Charter also examines the archival evidence, but notes in conclusion that it 'appears likely the rumours relating to the Elliston Massacre have a foundation in fact, and that some form of punitive action did take place on the cliffs at Waterloo Bay, upon which an exaggerated myth had developed'.[104]

What can we make of the fact that so many versions of the Elliston Incident exist? In everyday life, members of local communities – 'locals' – often distinguish themselves from outsiders by their access to stories of their district's past, stories that often feature local landmarks. In many rural communities in South Australia, and especially those either beyond the settled areas or on the margins between the settled and the unsettled, outsiders are known politely as 'tourists' or 'from town', less politely as 'rubbernecks' or 'terrorists'. Locals stress their sense of belonging to those communities by acknowledging their family connections with early settlement and through their possession of local legends (or by acknowledging their provenance). Typically locals will identify outsiders by their lack of access to the communal memory that is preserved in such local legends. It obviously helps if the legend is also associated with some dramatic local landform, like the cliffs to the south of Elliston. As A.T. Saunders notes in passing in the 1926 *Register* controversy, he had 'no doubt that that bold headland . . . at Waterloo Bay started the yarns'. The cliffs 'looked the right place for such a tragedy. It was a pity to waste such places, hence the yarns'.[105] Indeed, one of the authors of this book recalls a student describing her visit to the alleged site on the clifftops, and stressing the eerie and malevolent atmosphere of the place. Such feelings about some parts of the district were also recorded over a hundred years ago: Ellen Liston's character in her short story 'Doctor' describes 'a vast and terrible stillness [which] seemed to lie over everything; frequently it would press so heavily upon me that I was tempted to flee away shrieking as from some unholy presence'.[106]

Many rural communities still preserve local memories through their telling of local legends associated with local landforms. But as historian Pat Sumerling notes, with the passing of time and in the absence of written accounts (or their inaccessibility) by the 1920s the direct link with the foundation years of European settlement in South Australia was passing. In 1920 there would have been very few pioneers from 1836 still alive, let alone individuals who could clearly remember what happened in 1848 or 1849. Anyone in possession of a version of what happened at Elliston must have either known an adult participant or had access to local legends already in circulation, and obviously problems of hearsay evidence arise. As Sumerling says:

> Reminiscing in the 1920s, especially as South Australia headed for its first 100 years of European settlement, became a matter of urgency as early pioneers began to die. This prompted members of the rising generation to ask their elders what the pioneering days were like. Responses were often colourful, larger-than-life stories of frontier life. It was with much authority that some remembered 'something' about the massacre, with all its gory details as told to them by someone 'who was there'. . . . [T]he 1920s were ripe for the myth to grow and take root in a community at a time when age and memory were at their most precarious.[107]

The burgeoning numbers of local and family histories published since the 1960s has meant that increasingly such 'myths' are subjected to research, and if then written down often presented with the qualification that archival evidence may not exist that corroborates their details. The increasing scrutiny of the regional historical record has led to the challenging of the veracity of some local legends, a development often hotly contested by those who 'own' such stories and see their authority as storytellers undermined. A typical response to 'history' denying some versions of a well-polished yarn can be found in M.T. Bendall's Letter to the Adelaide *News* during the 1970 controversy over the Elliston massacre. He continues to insist (rather plaintively) in the face of the evidence that his father, F.W Farrant, *was* present in 1848, that dad *was* speared and carried the wounds to his grave, that there *were* 'bad' Aborigines in the district and that anyway his father *was* a friend of Archie Beviss, who knew the truth.[108]

In South Australia local legends that feature contact or conflict with Indigenous Australians are increasingly subject to investigation. Many have been reconsidered in the light of changing (or contested) communal attitudes to Indigenous political issues. Furthermore, contemporary sensitivities about the darker side of the pioneer legend may now mean that what was a common phenomenon until the

1960s – a swaggering amplification of a district's record of prejudice and violence – may now be qualified by those who would reject of such simple-minded vainglorious point-scoring. Our country was more violent than yours, is what those who told the Elliston massacre story really meant. Around here was the *real* Bush. *We* knew how to handle the 'Aboriginal Problem'.

One of the reasons why local legends are still told is because there have been relatively few attempts to write local histories until the last generation or so. Most of the hundreds of local and family histories have been published in the last 30 years, many of them appearing either in 1986 or in 1988, the years of the South Australian Sesquicentenary and the Australian Bicentenary celebrations. Of course some memoirs were written before the 1960s, but not many were known beyond the confines of those families (or districts) whose members might have written them. Often a typical rural district like the west coast was not so much country without history but country without historians. In such a district there is still a need for history, if only to separate the insiders from the outsiders, and local legends performed something of that social function. With the passing of time and the deaths of participants and eyewitnesses, details are blurred – or, paradoxically, details are sharpened, distorted, enlarged for narrative effect. Everyone likes a good yarn.

In many Indigenous communities a story is told of a group of Aboriginal people driven to their deaths over the cliffs just south of Elliston. A plan to erect a cairn on the cliffs south of Elliston was initiated in 1970 by the Federal Council for the Advancement of Aborigines and Torres Strait Islanders and the Aborigines Progress Association. According to the *Advertiser*, the memorial would 'commemorate a massacre of 250 aborigines by white settlers in 1846 [*sic*]' and was to have been 'part of a national mourning campaign by aborigines, coinciding with the Capt Cook centenary celebrations' planned for April 1970.[109] John Moriarty, assistant president of the South Australian Aborigines' Progress Association, was quoted as saying that the Elliston massacre was 'part of the history of the West Coast Aboriginal population despite strenuous efforts by the relatives of the whites involved to discredit what is a well-known fact'.[110] The chairman of the Elliston District Council, Mr J.B. Cameron, told the reporter that 'the council would agree to the cairn if it could be proved that the massacre took place'[111] and that a memorial to 'those Aborigines who lost their lives in the early development of the area' might be erected, presumably without any direct reference to the Waterloo Bay massacre. The *News* article has Cameron adding that 'we are unsure what happened back in 1848, and are hoping that someone can give us direction on the matter'.[112]

The news items in the Adelaide papers in 1970 provoked a predictable flurry of letters to the editor. Some correspondents like Norman Ford even claimed to have known Archie Beviss, who 'invented the Waterloo Bay massacre story, which was so completely exposed by the late Mr Somerville and Mr A.T. Saunders'.[113] Ford's letter provoked a quick response from Laurie Bryan, member of the Federal Council for the Advancement of Aborigines and Torres Strait Islanders:

> The racist tone of Norman Ford is greatly to be deplored.
>
> His claim about the Waterloo Bay massacre's [*sic*] being a myth is a personal opinion which is directly contrary to the opinions of the aboriginal people of the West Coast, who are basing their attitude on personal relationships with the aboriginal people involved in the incident.
>
> Having read most of Mr Summerville's [*sic*] research it is noteworthy that while he refers to atrocities by whites against blacks before 1839 (the date when Port Lincoln was first settled) he makes no mention of atrocities towards aboriginals after that date.
>
> He does make mention of atrocities against whites by aborigines.
>
> The last time Waterloo Bay was discussed was in 1929 when statements appeared such as: 'It is no good asking the niggers, because they have all gone where good niggers go.'
>
> If Europeans then and today were only prepared to ask aborigines their views it would clearly show that the situation is not as Mr Ford states.
>
> Some correspondents in 1929 were convinced the massacre occurred. Some were not.
>
> Australians voted ten to one in favour of aboriginal equality at the Aboriginal Rights Referendum. Our proposal is that those who voted for equality be invited to share in bringing it about.[114]

Bryan claims that 'the aboriginal people of the West Coast . . . [base] their attitude on personal relationships with the aboriginal people involved in the incident', clearly asserting an Indigenous oral history that links the 1840s with the 1970s, and insists that a massacre did occur at Elliston. Bryan's quoting of some of the details (and statements) from the 1920s newspaper controversies also suggests that at least some of the details in the Indigenous oral history may well have been drawn from a reading of those letters.

Pat Sumerling notes that in 1993 Aboriginal people were still telling the story:

> I asked a couple of local Aborigines . . . about their views of what happened near Elliston. They related that they were both told of a massacre that had taken place in the Elliston region where Aborigines had been chained together and thrown over the cliffs. As the Aboriginal oral tradition is of crucial importance to their culture, with stories handed down from generation to generation, one cannot dismiss their disturbing claims.[115]

On several occasions the authors of this book have discussed memories of the Elliston incident with Indigenous people in Ceduna and elsewhere on the coast. People have described how they will not visit Elliston, and one mentioned that he found stopping for petrol difficult. Although we have not heard Sumerling's detail about the victims being chained,[116] the broad particulars coincide: the site near Elliston; the numbers, about 250 rounded up and driven over the cliffs. We have heard one further detail: that not all the people died, the majority hiding at the base of the cliffs until the vigilantes left.

Poet and linguist Lee Cataldi notes that a version of the story has been collected in the Kimberleys in Western Australia by Charlie McAdam.[117] The fact that the story has travelled so far reveals the well-established political and social contacts between Indigenous communities that have developed since the 1970s. A flourishing oral history network now exists which has brought Indigenous Australians into contact with the local histories of their compatriots. Communities are sharing histories.

No memorial has ever been erected at Elliston. However, in December 1971 a plaque in memory of John Hamp marking the site of his death was unveiled by Mr P. Penna, deputy chairman of the Elliston District Council. It was nearly two years after the Adelaide newspaper controversy raged about the historical authenticity of the Elliston Massacre, two years after the Aboriginal community had not been allowed to erect a cairn at Elliston because there was no evidence of a massacre. The small granite memorial to Hamp can be read as an assertion of the truthfulness of the non-Indigenous version(s) of the legend, reinforcing the perception that the settlers only responded in the face of inexplicable, brutal and violent aggression by the Aborigines.[118] In the early 1970s P.J. Baillie made sure that most of the other sites pertaining to the Elliston incident were visited and either memorials erected or painted plates left to indicate their significance. At the sites of the Beevor and Easton huts, at the hanging tree at Taunto and at Easton's grave at Lake Hamilton (and, for good measure, at the grave of James Baird) either substantial granite cairns were built or (now fading) tin plates left describing what happened there, holding whitefella fragments of complex stories. Monuments such as these commemorate the European fallen of the Australian frontier. The Aboriginal dead remain uncommemorated.

Local legends such as the cluster that have been told about a putitive massacre near Elliston register the long and uneasy memories of violence in the unsettled areas of South Australia. Even if no massacre actually happened on a scale suggested by the detail of some versions, the obvious fact that people want to tell such a story reveals a deep

P.J. Ballie's memorial to Annie Easton
(photograph by Rick Hosking)

unease about the communal memory of frontier history. Some people may tell the story as a way of demonstrating sympathy for and solidarity with the Indigenous victims of colonialism, while others may tell it as a way of boasting about how bold, resolute and resourceful were the early settlers who took the law into their own hands. As time has passed, however, the telling of such stories for whatever motive uncovers that 'dark unholy presence' revealed in the stories that are inscribed on the sunny walls of the Elliston Community Agricultural Hall. Whether we Australians like it or not, the Indigenous presence is at the centre of our communal memory. The doubts, fears and hopes that we experience as a nation are often to do with the presence and the futures of Indigenous Australians. Such stories as those told about the cliffs of Waterloo Bay have become 'narrative battlegrounds in which conscience . . . [fights] itself into a kind of consciousness'.[119]

THE LEGEND OF
JAMES BROWN

∎

James Brown arrived in South Australia with his brother Archibald in May 1839. The following year, the brothers established a property called Allendale in the Encounter Bay district. James struck out on his own in 1849, and took out a lease on 178 square kilometres of land, which he called Avenue Range Station. By the mid-1860s Brown's holdings had grown to 470 square kilometres and, in the words of his biographer, 'he prospered exceedingly'. Rodney Cockburn's entry for Brown in *The Pastoral Pioneers of South Australia* portrays him as a great benefactor:

> Considering that those two great charitable institutions – the Kalyra Consumptive Sanatorium at Belair and Estcourt House near the Grange – were founded in his memory, and out of the proceeds of his estate, surprisingly little publicity has been devoted to the career of James Brown, a pioneer of the South-Eastern district.[1]

Later in the sketch Cockburn offers a rather perfunctory explanation for this lack of publicity:

> Very early in his career he received a severe setback by becoming involved in a charge of poisoning a blackfellow, but emerged from the trial with a clean escutcheon, a jury of his fellow countrymen finding him not guilty. He was not the only pioneer pastoralist who had to undergo a similar ordeal, but it was probably this incident which accounted for the meagre publicity associated with his name both before and after his death.[2]

Cockburn goes on to defend Brown's reputation, arguing that the incident he had been involved in was part and parcel of 'the circumstances

James Brown as reproduced in Rodney Cockburn,
Pastoral Pioneers of South Australia, Publisher's Limited, 1927

and conditions of the day', and that he deserves respect as a 'pastoral pathfinder' who 'suffered at the hands of untamed blacks, who not only menaced the white man even to the point of murder, but speared and scattered their flocks at will, to the great detriment of the industry'.[3]

Brown may have suffered 'meagre publicity' but he was by no means forgotten. Stories about his involvement in the murder of Aborigines became part of the frontier folklore of South Australia's south-east. The most commonly told version of the story appears to be an elaboration of the Cockburn account.

In 1944 a local historian, J.G. Hastings, recorded a more elaborate account of the poisoning incident in which Brown had allegedly been involved. Under the heading, 'The Poisoning of Blacks on Avenue Range Station', Hastings writes:

> There is no mention of this affair in the Police records at the Adelaide Archives, but the story is recorded here as it was told to me by old residents of the South-East who knew the chief actor. It is not known just when the tragedy took place, but it may have been at any time between 1860–70.[4]

In this account, Brown is said to have suffered from repeated depredations on his sheep and cattle by the local Aborigines. 'Driven to the limit of desperation', Brown decided to take the law into his own hands. He laced a quantity of flour with arsenic and placed it within the Aborigines' reach, certain that they would not be able to resist the temptation of stealing the flour and eating it. This done, he set about making his alibi:

> He owned a fine horse, noted for its great powers of endurance. He immediately saddled and mounted it, and steered a course for the sea coast without delay. He then followed the beach for about 90 miles to the Murray Mouth. After swimming across he rode straight for Adelaide and arrived there somewhere between the second and third day. In the meantime the flour had done its work and the news was spread about. A large number of natives of both sexes, young and old alike, were found dead along the shore of the swamp.[5]

When the police investigated the deaths and 'Jimmy' was called to account for his movements, 'his horse's great performance stood him in good stead'. 'It was claimed at the trial that it was utterly impossible for Brown to do the deed and then ride to Adelaide, where he appeared immediately afterwards.' Hastings' account concludes on the sentimental note that Brown, 'out of gratitude', turned his horse loose in the best feed and never allowed him to be ridden again as long as he lived.[6]

Aboriginal people also tell the story. Colleagues of ours were told the story in 1987 by an elderly Aboriginal man from Kingston. Jimmy Brown, he said, had shot some Aboriginal people and poisoned others with strychnine in their flour. The reason was that they were stealing his sheep. Brown 'got off', he said, because a horse ride to Adelaide established his alibi.[7] Some months after this oral version was recorded, Hastings' account was reproduced verbatim in a local history entitled *The Coorong and Lakes of the Lower Murray*, by Tom McCourt and Hans Mincham.[8]

Hastings' story appeared again in 1990 in an Aboriginal Studies book for secondary students published by the South Australian Education Department.[9] It was used in a section dealing with frontier violence and was prefaced with the following remarks:

> As late as the 1860s resistance and violence was still occurring. The following account of unknown origin, written in the 1930s, describes action taken against Aboriginal people who had attacked stock. It is written from a European perspective. An Aboriginal perspective follows it.[10]

Hastings' account was reproduced verbatim and followed by an Aboriginal version told by a Ngarrindjeri man whose family comes from the area where Brown established his property.[11] This account begins by describing the way Aboriginal people were used as cheap labour and were paid with flour and sugar. When 'lean times' came during a drought, the Aborigines would sneak in and steal some of the rations from the store. The station owner, presumably Brown although he is not named, 'got sick of it' and laced some of the flour with arsenic before getting on his horse and riding full pelt to Adelaide. While he was doing so, the Aborigines stole the flour, took it back to their camp and almost everyone who ate it died. The story concludes with the observation that the authorities knew who had done it but it could not be proved because he was in Adelaide at the time.[12] The versions are quite similar, the notable difference being that while Hastings portrays

Brown as the victim of Aboriginal aggressions, the Aboriginal accounts put the emphasis on white exploitation.

Hastings prefaced his account with a claim that there was no mention of the affair in the police records in the Adelaide archives. The incident James Brown was involved in, however, is quite well documented, not only by the police but by the protector of Aborigines, a local magistrate, the Adelaide press and the advocate general. But the documented incident is very different from the stories that have survived in local tradition.

Sometime in January 1849 reports were received that some Aborigines had been murdered near Guichen Bay in the south-east. Protector of Aborigines Matthew Moorhouse was ordered to visit the district and investigate the allegations. Moorhouse arrived on 19 February and began his investigation several days later in the company of three men: Corporal Burgon, an interpreter and an Aboriginal guide. They were taken to the scene of the crime by Leandermin, an Aboriginal man who had witnessed the murders.[13]

Leandermin described what he saw. He and a European named Parker had been travelling along the road when they heard shots fired. He went to investigate and, from the cover of trees, saw four or five native women lying dead on the ground, their wounds 'fresh and bleeding'. There were others on the ground whom Leandermin presumed were dead because they were not moving. Two white men were present at the scene; Brown was identified as one of them and had a gun in his hand.[14]

The protector examined the area and found five holes that had human remains in them. Near these graves, they found 'human bones scattered in every direction' and paper that had been discharged from a gun: 'We continued our examination of the ground for some time, and discovered, about 80 paces from the graves, the remains of a fire, amongst which were portions of calcined bones'.[15] It was the protector's opinion that the bodies had first been buried but were later exhumed and burnt in an effort to destroy any evidence. Exactly when the murders had occurred is not clear. In his original report, Moorhouse simply notes that they had occurred some months before; in his published report, he suggests 'about September' of 1848.[16] In a summary of the case, written several months after the protector's report appeared, the advocate general indicated that it was 'about November'.[17] Whatever the exact time, at least two months had passed before the case was investigated.

James Brown was charged with murder on 1 March 1849. In late March or early April he appeared before a local magistrate, Captain Butler, who committed him for trial. Butler had little doubt of Brown's guilt. Writing to a friend in Adelaide, he listed the victims: one 'old man blind and infirm', three female adults, two teenage girls (one of 15 and one of 12), and three female children (one of 18 months, one of two years and a babe in arms). There was, he added, 'little question of the butchery or of the butcher'.[18]

Brown's trial 'for murder of unknown aboriginal natives' came before the Supreme Court in Adelaide on 11 June 1849. The judge was not convinced that the evidence presented was sufficient to sustain the case. Laws pertaining to Aboriginal evidence allowed unsworn Aboriginal testimony to be accepted in court, but with a number of powerful caveats. In the first instance, it was left to the court to judge the 'weight and credibility of the evidence' and, more importantly, in cases where the punishment was death or transportation, the unsworn testimony of an 'uncivilised person or persons' was deemed to be insufficient unless corroborated by other evidence.[19] The judge would not bring the case on unless further evidence was presented. When the case was again brought before the court a week later, the judge was still not convinced that the evidence was sufficient. Nonetheless, given that 'great suspicion rested on the case', he gave the prosecution more time to prepare, and Brown was released on bail of £500.[20]

Toward the end of July 1849, the advocate general summed up the status of the investigation. Parker, who had witnessed the crime in the company of Leandermin, 'denied all knowledge of the matter', as did others who were said to have heard the matter discussed in Brown's presence. Brown's accomplice, the stockkeeper Eastwood, alias Yorky, absconded when the investigation began and was reported to have left the colony aboard a 'South Sea Whaler off Kangaroo Island'. Joice, described as a material witness in the case, had gone to the Port Phillip district. The principal Aboriginal witness, Leandermin, who, it appears, was being detained at Guichen Bay, absconded and was 'supposed to have been made away with'. Of those witnesses who could be persuaded to attend, 'all more or less connected with the prisoner, it was apparent that they were determined to give no evidence to impeach him'.[21] The prosecution's task seemed hopeless but the advocate general ordered that the investigation continue and issued warrants for the apprehension of the fugitives in neighbouring colonies. Brown again appeared before the criminal sittings of the Supreme Court on 10 and 28 September and the judge again refused to hear the case without fresh evidence.[22] By the November sittings, Brown's name had disappeared from the calendar of the court.[23] This was the end of the matter as far as the authorities were concerned. Despite the fact that the people involved in investigating the case had no doubt of Brown's guilt, settler solidarity and legal technicalities meant that he was never even put on trial.

During Brown's lifetime there was only one published recounting of the Avenue Range massacre and this was discretely tucked away in Christina Smith's 1880 missionary tract, *The Booandik Tribe of South Australian Aborigines*. Her account is as interesting for what it omits as for what it reveals. Christina Smith was a devout Presbyterian who arrived with her husband at Rivoli Bay in the south-east in 1845. Settlement of the region had only recently commenced and violence was a constant feature of frontier life.[24] The first stories she heard when she arrived in the district concerned 'troublesome blacks' and so it is no surprise to read in her diary: 'I hardly enjoyed a full night's sleep for six weeks after landing – dreading they might attack us in the night'. When the Aborigines first appeared at her hut – 'in a friendly manner', she recalled – her husband approached them while she stood in the background with a gun in hand.[25]

Smith took a maternal interest in the welfare of the Aborigines, especially the 'half-caste and orphan' children, some of whom she took into her home and raised with her own children. Although Smith was not a trained missionary and was not sponsored by any missionary society, her interest continued and, in 1865, she opened an 'Aborigines Home' at Mount Gambier. The home received some financial assistance from the Bishop of Adelaide and the government provided rations for the residents but a high mortality rate from disease, particularly measles, resulted in closure in 1867.[26]

Smith's account of the Buandig is divided into two sections: the first is a brief ethnographic account of the people, and the second a series of 'memoirs' describing the lives of some of the Aborigines she knew at Rivoli Bay and Mount Gambier. One of these memoirs concerns an Aboriginal boy named Wergon, or Peter, whom she adopted while still at Rivoli Bay in the 1840s. Smith proudly relates how Wergon converted to Christianity and would occasionally go out and spread the gospel among his people.[27] One of these journeys took him into the territory of the 'Wattatonga tribe' – a group whose land encompassed James Brown's newly established Avenue Range station. Wergon returned after a week and reported 'the massacre of eleven of the tribe he had visited, by two white men'.[28] Wergon persuaded a witness to the events, a youth whose parents had apparently been killed in the massacre, to return with him to Rivoli Bay. According to Wergon's account, 'the white men had shown no mercy to either the grey-headed old man or to the helpless infant on its mother's breast', and the motive for the massacre was the killing of sheep 'belonging to a settler in the Guichen Bay district'.

Smith does not name the settler, nor the accomplice mentioned, but this is not surprising – Brown was alive and well and still living in the district when her book appeared. It might explain why Smith is rather coy about the details of the massacre, mentioning twice that there were eleven victims but never describing the manner of their deaths. She does indicate, however, that the bodies of the victims were burnt. Regarding the fate of the murderers, she writes: 'The case was taken up by the authorities, but discharged for want of evidence'. Smith comments that, had the murderers been 'natives', she has no doubt that sufficient evidence would have been found or 'less conclusive evidence would have been deemed sufficient to justify a sentence of death'. She concludes by observing that on 'the day of retribution the judge will be an impartial one' and the 'real criminals' will face the 'torments of the eternal fire'.[29] Smith wrote about the event because she wanted the atrocity remembered but was understandably cautious of publicly levelling allegations against a prominent member of her community.

The contemporary evidence shows that James Brown and his hutkeeper were probably responsible for the shooting murder of at least nine people in 1848. The only published recounting of these events produced in Brown's lifetime, while understandably circumspect, corroborated the essential details. How is it, then, that the folk memory of the Avenue Range massacre concerns a poisoning and an heroic horse ride?

The first and most obvious question is whether we are dealing with the same event? Was Brown involved in two (or more) massacres? While this cannot be absolutely ruled out, evidence suggests that the stories about Brown that circulated after his death in 1890 were all elaborations of the 1848 killings. In the first place, court records indicate that Brown was arrested on only one occasion, for the shooting murders committed near his station in 1848. There is no recorded scuttle-butt suggesting that he had been involved in other killings, at least not until the poisoning story was put to paper by Cockburn in the 1920s. It might reasonably be countered that the poisoning was another event that went officially unreported. If this is so, what must be explained is how the accounts of Cockburn and Hastings, and most of the subsequent versions, stressed the fact that Brown was tried for his involvement in the massacre. Hastings' version, for instance, was built around the horse-ride alibi confounding the prosecution at his trial.

Hastings dated the poisoning episode to some time between 1860 and 1870, a decade or more after the 1848 incident. The date, however, is highly unlikely. Frontier violence in the district began with the arrival of squatters in 1843 and was petering out by 1848.[30] By 1852, when the Victorian goldrush was under way, pastoralists were actively seeking Aboriginal workers to fill the void left by the exodus of European labour.[31] In fact, the murders by Brown and Yorky in 1848 were one of the last serious frontier episodes to be documented in the district. On this point, most of the frontier clashes, including one in which eight Aborigines were reported to have been killed, occurred before James Brown had settled in the area.[32] Yet none of these has survived in the recorded folklore of the district. In colonial South Australia relatively few Europeans were charged with the murder of Aborigines, and no one was charged with a poisoning murder.[33] So where did the poisoning element of the story come from?

There are strong suspicions that settlers used poison as a tool of murder in the south-east. In the 1840s the region was regarded as particularly violent. Evelyn Sturt, a local pastoralist and magistrate, in 1846 listed a number of atrocities that he believed had occurred in the district and added: 'I believe a wholesale system of murder has been carried on which it is most difficult to obtain any evidence of'.[34] In 1844 the government became concerned at reports of violence in the district, and Sergeant Major Alford was ordered to investigate. According to the police commissioner:

> The Sergeant Major learnt from another person on his way home, as a rumour, that the natives of the Rivoli Bay District and Glenelg have generally been treated in a manner which can only be called atrocious if true. It was stated to him that damper poisoned with corrosive sublimate was given them.[35]

Christina Smith recorded a story of the Aborigines' first encounter with sheep and cattle near Salt Creek. A party visited the white men's camp and were given some mutton and damper to eat. The women who told Christina Smith the story recalled that 'we tasted the mutton, and found it very good; but we buried the damper, as we were afraid of being poisoned'.[36]

An entirely separate incident, which occurred on the colony's western frontier, may have a bearing on the James Brown story. On 15 May 1849 the police at Port Lincoln received information that some Aborigines had been poisoned near the town's mine. The story was that a local shepherd, Patrick Dwyer, annoyed at having flour stolen from his hut, laced some of his supply with arsenic. The flour was subsequently stolen and eight Aborigines became sick after eating it and five died. Dwyer was arrested on suspicion but was released shortly afterwards for want of sufficient evidence. The protector travelled to the district in July 1849 and investigated the case. He examined the flour bag at the camp where the Aborigines had died and found traces of arsenic in it. It is likely that Dwyer would have been arrested for murder had he not fled the district and sailed to California.[37] This is one of the better-known poisoning incidents in colonial South Australia, and it occurred a month after Brown's arrest for murder. Details of the episode were discussed in the press at the same time that Brown's case was before the Supreme Court.

In summary, while there is no evidence to link Brown with the poisoning of Aborigines, there is evidence that poisonings had occurred in the south-east, at least prior to his arrival. Furthermore, a major poisoning case involving Aborigines, but in the Port Lincoln district, occurred at the same time that Brown's case was before the court and was a matter of public interest. It is a possibility that the two incidents became mixed in folk memory or, more simply, that local stories of poisoning circulated in the south-east in later years and became associated with the Avenue Range incident.

What of the horse ride? Given that Brown and Yorky shot their victims dead, and the crime was not discovered until some months later, an epic horse ride up the Coorong to Adelaide to establish an alibi makes no sense. Part of the explanation may lie in another account of the episode that appeared three years after James Brown's death.

Simpson Newland's novel *Paving the Way, a Romance of the Australian Bush* was published in 1893. The novel is a saga of South Australian settlement that tells the story, in large measure, by fictionalising actual events. The events, writes Newland, though 'romantic, are mainly authentic'.³⁸ Much of what he writes about is set in country he knew, and incorporates characters and events with which he was familiar. Newland was still a child when his family arrived in Australia in 1839, his father establishing a pastoral property near Encounter Bay shortly afterwards. Growing up in the south-east, Newland became acquainted with many of the local Aboriginal people and, in later years, wrote about them with considerable sympathy.³⁹ One of the fictionalised accounts in the novel was James Brown's story. The novel's hero, Roland Grantley, took the part of Brown, while the character Darkie – a white man – stood in for Brown's overseer, Yorky. Newland begins by explaining the hardships the pioneers faced in their efforts to establish themselves on the land. In the absence of police protection, Newland explains, the vulnerable settler sometimes had no choice but to take the law into his own hands when the lives of his men and his stock were threatened.

The district in which Grantley establishes his run is in an unsettled state with constant attacks on shepherds and the destruction of stock. After an attack on one of their shepherds, Grantley and Darkie decide that it is useless to seek assistance so they 'determine to follow up the marauders alone, and to take such vengeance as should deter them from committing any more of these outrages'.⁴⁰ In the events that follow, it is Darkie, with his bush experience, who takes the leading part. They track the Aborigines to their hiding place, where they are said to be 'amusing themselves' by killing the sheep. With a shout of 'Slay and spare not', both men begin firing into the camp: 'Ten or a dozen were killed and many more wounded before a halt was made'. Returning to the scene that evening, they make a pyre of wood, corpses and carcasses and set it ablaze.⁴¹

At this time, the narrator continues, reports begin to filter back to the authorities that 'many blacks had been shot in a cold-blooded and remorseless manner, in consequence of the supineness with which the squatters' demands for protection had been treated'.⁴² It is rumoured that the government wants to make 'an example' of one of the settlers in an attempt to suppress the violence. A detachment of police is sent to the district to investigate reports of the massacre. Having heard rumours of this on the grapevine, Darkie decides it is better to flee rather than risk implicating his boss. As an 'old hand', Darkie is able to

Herbert Cole, 'Darkie saw his pursuers grow less and less',
from Simpson Newland, *Paving the Way: A Romance of the
Australian Bush*, Drexel Biddle, Philadelphia, 1899

Herbert Cole, 'Without the smallest repugnance or concern he
began piling up dried wood, dead black men, and defunct sheep in
a heap together', from Simpson Newland, *Paving the Way:
A Romance of the Australian Bush*, Drexel Biddle, Philadelphia, 1899

call upon the 'freemasonry that existed' amongst his class to find his way to Kangaroo Island where he can find passage on a whaling ship and leave the colony.[43] Grantley, grateful for his man's help, lets Darkie have his prize horse, Star, to make his escape. With troopers in hot pursuit, Darkie flees along the Coorong, swims with his horse across the mouth of the Murray River, and eludes his pursuers. Grantley is arrested for the crime but, without the evidence of the overseer, authorities decide not to proceed with the case.[44]

Newland's fictional account records most of the key details of the 1848 killings. The victims were shot, their bodies burnt, the hutkeeper fled the colony on a whaling vessel when an investigation began, and the principal actor was arrested but released for want of evidence. Newland got the context right as well. In 1849 the government conducted a crack-down on settlers suspected of using violence against the Aborigines. More Europeans appeared before the Supreme Court for crimes against the Aborigines in that year than in any other of the nineteenth century. All the accused were found not guilty or were released without trial.[45] Nonetheless, as Newland wrote:

> A revulsion of feeling in favour of the black men had set in, and it was understood that, if a white man was charged with the murder of a black, it would go hard on him, if the case was moderately strong.[46]

Quite accurately, Newland also documents the feeling among settlers that they were forced to take the law into their own hands because the government provided them with inadequate protection. As a Port Lincoln settler wrote to the *Register* in September 1849:

> At Port Lincoln and Yorke's Peninsula the natives have been robbing, murdering, and mutilating the whites for the last twelve months, as if they were opossums instead of human beings. Yet the moment a white inflicts retributive justice, which the Government had denied, he is immediately pounced upon by a horde of distinction-seekers, dragged manacled hundreds of miles to Adelaide, and confronted with a batch of cannibal urchins who have no idea of either the nature of the proceedings, or of truth, or of evidence, beyond mumbling out 'yes,' through an interpreter, to every leading question that the 'eager maker-up of the case' chooses to ask.[47]

Newland makes no effort to gloss over the settler's actions; the massacre and the disposal of the bodies is described in graphic detail. However, he immediately diverts the reader's attention from the atrocity with a thrilling description of Darkie's dramatic ride to freedom.

While later versions of the James Brown story such as Hastings' account might have borrowed from Newland, or perhaps from garbled retellings of his account, it is still not clear where the horse-ride story itself came from. Newland may simply have invented it as a plot device. On the other hand, Yorky did have to get to Encounter Bay to board the whaling vessel that took him out of the colony, and it is quite possible that he did so by riding a horse up the Coorong, impelled by the fear that he might be arrested for the crime he had committed. However, there are further possibilities contained in other versions of the story.

In 1939, Clement Smith, Independent member for the state seat of Victoria, which encompassed most of the south-east, made reference to the James Brown case when making a speech in parliament. Smith was a pastoralist from Kingston, quite close to where the massacre had taken place 90 years before. The speech was given in a debate on a proposed Aborigines Act that would, among other things, introduce a system of exemptions that sought to encourage Aboriginal people to 'pass' into the general community as 'honorary whites'. Smith opposed the bill and, in doing so, prefaced his argument with a potted history of the treatment of Aborigines in South Australia. 'The story', he said, 'was a very pathetic one' and he proceeded to give an example:

> In one instance many natives were slaughtered at Keleira. These men had been harassing sheep flocks. Many years ago I saw large quantities of the bones of those natives when crossing the swamps where they were shot down. A reference will be found to that in 'Paving the Way'. The man who rode from Keleira Station to report to the police was James Brown. He could not find his horse and after a frantic search of more than two hours he mounted a 14.1 chestnut pony and leaving Keleira homestead at 10 a.m. he reported to police headquarters in Adelaide the following morning, having in the course of that trip swum the River Murray. The journey by his horse constitutes an outstanding feat of equine endurance.[48]

So perhaps the horse ride was originally nothing more than a desperate effort by Brown to avoid breaching bail conditions that required him to regularly report to the police. There are other points worthy of note in this account. While Smith set out to use the story as an illustration of frontier violence against Aborigines, it is as if he could not help himself and turned it into an account of a pioneer's heroic horse ride. Furthermore, the victims in this account were not poisoned but were shot down.

Versions of the James Brown story have been a common feature of local histories about the south-east from the 1950s onwards and the focus of most of these was on the horse ride. James Brown's story was retold in Elma Smith's *History of Kingston* in 1950. She writes that Brown was 'ruthless in his treatment of marauding natives who harassed his sheep flocks', and continues:

> The penalty imposed upon him required him to report periodically to Police Headquarters in Adelaide. On one occasion he was unable to find his horses for the long journey; for one and a half days a feverish search was made for the missing animals. In despair Brown mounted a dark chestnut station pony and commenced his record ride to Adelaide, swimming his pony across the Murray. Leaving Keleira in the morning, he had breakfast in Adelaide the next morning, and duly reported at 10 am.[49]

This account avoids the original crime entirely and glosses over the court case by referring to the penalty imposed upon Brown of periodically having to report to police headquarters in Adelaide. It does, however, play up the desperate horse ride on an inadequate animal and the swim across the Murray, an element that dates back to Simpson Newland's novel.

Another variation of James Brown's exploits was published in 1970 in *Kingston Flashback*, written by local historian Verne McLaren. What appears to have been originally one story is now split into two. By way of introduction, McLaren writes of some 'unsavoury stories associated with Brown which have been handed down in the district'.[50] The first of these was that the Aborigines acquired a 'taste for mutton' and stole and mutilated Brown's sheep. Brown, writes McLaren, 'would have none of this and the handed-down version is that he poisoned flour, which the natives filched and many deaths were the result'. End of poisoning story: no arrest, no trial, no heroic horse ride. McLaren then tells another story:

On his property were the Papineau Caves in which natives lived. An accomplice and Brown, it is said, on one occasion smoked the natives out and as they ran, shot them. The natives would never attempt to kill Brown as he was considered an evil spirit – apparently evil spirits were spared spears.

Eventually the law catches up with Brown and he is charged with the murder. The case is not proven, though the authorities try for a year, during which time he is obliged to report periodically to Police Headquarters in Adelaide.[51]

As might be guessed, the account ends with Brown desperately trying to find a horse, making do with a pony and commencing 'his famous ride, swimming the Murray en route'. This is the first time that the story of Aboriginal people being smoked out of the Papineau Caves appeared – eighty years after James Brown's death and more than 120 years after the Avenue Range massacre – but, from this point onwards, it becomes part of 'James Brown' folklore.

Barry Durman, another local historian, published a book in 1978 entitled *A History of the Baker's Range Settlement*. The section devoted to James Brown includes a short history of his association with the Avenue Range, or Keleira, property and contains an account of the massacre, or massacres, with which Brown was associated. Durman deals with the 1848 episode with scissors and paste by simply quoting a contemporary newspaper account of Brown's arrest. The article, which appeared in the *Southern Australian* on 20 March 1849, reported that Brown had been committed for trial for the murder of five Aborigines, that the evidence against him was 'fearfully conclusive', and that a box full of bones was being brought to Adelaide to be produced as evidence. The manner of the victims' deaths, which was not indicated in the newspaper report, is passed over by Durman, who remarks merely that Brown was remanded on bail and later discharged.[52] Durman then goes on to tell another story about James Brown, never attempting to make clear whether it is a variation of the story he has already related or something quite different. He writes:

A story handed down over the years, recounts a wonderful feat of horsemanship by Mr Brown. It is a pity that it varies from different tale-tellers, but one version, generally accepted relates how, after smoking out and shooting fleeing natives from the Papineau

Caves, Brown was arraigned on charges of murder which were not proven, despite the authorities persisting for a year.[53]

Durman reintroduces the issue of the horse's fate – it is now a horse again and not a chestnut pony – when he concludes: 'The horse, in later years, is said to have died of old age at 10 mile point, now known as Taratap'.[54] Durman's final sentence about the horse dying of old age echoes of J.G. Hastings' sentimental yarn that the horse was left out to pasture as a reward for its services.

When Hastings recorded his version of the story in the 1940s, he anticipated doubters and warned them that there was 'no mention of this affair in the Police records at the Adelaide Archives' and that it was told to him 'by old residents of the South-East who knew the chief actor'. He is stressing the fact that it is a local tradition. Indeed, most of the versions published over time include comments that the story has been 'handed down', or 'told to me by'. But this by no means excludes the possibility that those who have told the story have also read it, or been told the story by someone who has read it. When Clement Smith told his version in parliament in 1936, he noted that Simpson Newland had recorded it in *Paving the Way*. This quintessential novel of the South Australian frontier has circulated widely and been republished often since 1893. This is an oral tradition in a predominantly literate society.

One of the other ways in which the storytellers have attempted to give veracity to the yarn is by linking it to the local landscape. Clement Smith, for instance, recalled how he had seen the bones of the victims in the swamp where they were killed. While he may well have seen bones, they were unlikely to have been those of Brown's victims because these had been gathered as evidence by the protector, and it is highly unlikely that they were returned to the spot. While earlier accounts vaguely locate the incident at a 'swamp' on Brown's property, later versions associate the massacre with a named feature of the local landscape – the Papineau Caves. While reference to the caves is a recent innovation in the evolution of the James Brown story, associative landmarks are often important in local traditions. Historian David Roberts draws attention to the interdependence between story and landmark in the mythology surrounding the 'Bells Falls massacre' in New South Wales: discussion of the Bells Falls Gorge, he notes, elicited accounts of the massacre, while talk of Aborigines or massacres resulted in references to the gorge.[55] Chris Healy has also noted that 'post-invasion physical reference points' have often been integral to local history discussions of Aborigines.[56] Such associations not only appear to provide 'proof', but operate as a mnemonic, anchoring the event in social memory by inscribing it on the landscape.

The question of whether Brown was involved in two 'incidents', a shooting that was investigated by the authorities and a poisoning that was not, requires further comment in connection with the issue of oral traditions. We have argued that it was unlikely that there were two separate incidents because Brown's appearance in court was the unifying element in both, and he only appeared before the courts for the shooting murders. Reasons have been offered why the poisoning element might have become incorporated into the story. The fact remains that he may have been involved in two incidents – there is an oral tradition to that effect – but there is no positive evidence that Brown was involved in a poisoning. On the other hand, there is positive evidence that Brown was involved in shooting murders. Furthermore, even if you accept that both events occurred, the effect of the 'pioneer' transformation of the story remains the same. By the twentieth century, Brown is not remembered for committing an atrocity, he is not reviled in the stories as a murderer – he is remembered, pre-eminently, as the man who undertook an epic horse ride.

The two recorded Aboriginal versions of the story substantially repeat the European account – focusing on Brown's alleged involvement in a poisoning rather than shooting murders. It is likely that there was a quite different version of the story circulating among the Aboriginal community of the south-east in the years immediately after the massacre. After all, there was an Aboriginal witness to the events and, at the time, Aboriginal people throughout the south-east would have known full well the details of the atrocity that Brown committed. We know that this was so in the European community. Christina Smith's account makes it apparent that the details of the case were still known in 1880, and it was still fresh enough in Simpson Newland's mind to become an episode in *Paving the Way*.

With the passage of time the James Brown story was transformed from a cold-blooded shooting to a sly poisoning and heroic horse ride. It is difficult to make a hero out of someone who shoots defenceless men, women and children. Poisoning, on the other hand, is a more passive 'set and forget' type of crime, one in which the victims are complicit in their own demise through the act of stealing the flour. As we have seen, there was a major poisoning story being reported, quite coincidentally, at the time of the Avenue Range killings, and others probably circulated as part of the frontier folklore of the south-east. By focusing on poisoning, rather than shooting, the received story plays down the level of the atrocity.

The alibi-setting horse ride, on the other hand, shifted the focus of the story entirely. The murder of Aboriginal people ceased to be the subject of the story and became a plot device, setting up the description of an heroic horse ride up the Coorong and across the mouth of the Murray. In more recent accounts the poisoning element of the story became secondary; indeed, it became a second story, replaced by a massacre of Aboriginal people as they were smoked out of caves – but the horse ride remained central. For the European tellers, it was a story about the skill, enterprise and gumption of the pioneer. Accounts of Brown's involvement in the shooting murders on Avenue Range station circulated until about the turn of the century but were eventually erased from the social memory of both the black and white communities. The mechanism of erasure was the filter of the pioneer legend. That stories like the one of James Brown evolved as they did, and circulated virtually uncontested, is testament to the influence of the 'pioneer legend' in shaping White Australia's view of the past.

FATAL COLLISIONS IN THE FLINDERS RANGES

■

In 1852 Robert Richardson, a young Irishman from Dublin, was one of Johnson Frederick Hayward's shepherds on Aroona in the Flinders Ranges, the most northerly run in the South Australian colony. On 14 March he was murdered by Aborigines at Youngoona (or Yunguna) Hut about nine kilometres (five miles) to the south-east of 'Government House', the Aroona head station. Richardson's murder was one of the relatively small number of fatal collisions on the Flinders Ranges frontier: it is commonly held that conflict between settlers and Aboriginal people was not as widespread in the far north as it was in other parts of the colony.[1]

There are a number of representations of the Richardson murder that survive in a range of different genres: government records, newspaper accounts, published and unpublished memoirs, tourist guidebooks and two works of fiction. Each representation contributes to a popular historical archive of local legends, yarns, generalities, fragments of historical fact, silences, erasures, fabrications, misconceptions and selective reminiscence that constitutes the communal memory of the early years of European invasion and occupation of the far north. Reading the archive offers insights into the selective social functions of local historical memory. Richardson's murder – if remembered at all – is usually seen as a sad and atypical consequence of unfortunate frontier violence in the roaring days. The 'collision' provoked by the murder is hardly remembered at all. The site of the murder at Youngoona is now a tourist destination in the Flinders Ranges National Park just off the track out of Brachina Gorge heading for Wilpena. No attempt has yet been made to memorialise the events of 1852 save for a line or two in guidebooks and a line drawing in a bushwalker's strip map.

News of the Richardson murder reached the authorities in Adelaide in a letter to the colonial secretary's office dated 2 April 1852 from the Clare justice of the peace, J.B. Hughes. While briefly reporting the murder, the letter also noted that there were policing difficulties in the north caused by the closing of the Mount Remarkable police station because of the general exodus of South Australian men to the Victorian gold diggings. Hughes reported the absence of magistrates north of Clare, urging the government to 'appoint some Magistrate residing in the neighbourhood'. The letter is annotated by C.M. Stuart for the commissioner of police, revealing that Corporal Coward and Police Constable Harvey were instructed to leave Adelaide immediately to reopen the Mount Remarkable police station.[2] The implication is that the likelihood of further 'outrages' occurring would be diminished by an appropriate police presence and sworn magistrates residing in the district. It is further implied that 'sheepholders' and their employees have acted and will continue to act outside the law unless the 'efficiency' of policing is improved. The swift action by the commissioner suggests that he concurred.

Hughes' letter was accompanied by one from station owner Johnson Frederick ('Fred') Hayward reporting the murder of his employee Robert Richardson. Hayward's revelations are stark: allegations of murder levelled against 'the Natives'; attempts at arrest of suspects; a clear admission that he had 'been compelled to protect [his] . . . men, & and in the attempt to capture, to fire on the murderers in self defence', all justified, it seems, by the absence of police from the district. Hayward admits that there was a collision between settlers and the Indigenous people of the Flinders (the Adnyamathanha or Yura), a collision provoked by Richardson's murder. He acknowledges that he and his men had taken the law into their own hands but he is coy about casualties.

As the ensuing correspondence to and from the colonial secretary's office makes clear, there was considerable interest in the circumstances surrounding Richardson's murder, the events the murder had precipitated and the circumstances of Billy and Jemmy, the two suspects eventually arrested for that murder. The first letter, from the resident magistrate at Kooringa, James W. Macdonald, to the advocate general, enquires how long suspects might be detained on suspicion of murder.[3] As becomes obvious in a subsequent letter dated 14 April 1852, Macdonald was particularly concerned about two aspects of the case. First, he considered the police evidence against the suspects 'not very strong', based as it was on the 'length and breadth with the tracks found about the corpse of the murdered man as measured by Mr Hayward' and on the recovery of stolen sheepskins and part of a shirt.[4] Hayward himself had collected this evidence and made it available to Sergeant Major Rose when he arrived at Aroona to conduct the investigation. Second, Macdonald repeats his request for advice from the advocate general about how long he might remand the suspects in custody. He notes that given the state of the northern districts, with passions running high, he feared 'evil consequences' if the prisoners were liberated too soon.[5]

On 16 April 1852 the *Register* reported the first appearance of the prisoners in the Local Court at Clare before magistrate Macdonald. The court heard that Richardson had been 'speared in the spine and loins', suggesting that he might have been murdered as payback for a sexual offence or for failing to practice reciprocity, perhaps for failing to provide goods for sexual favours received.

Hayward came down from Aroona to give evidence and described in the witness box how he 'found the foot prints of three bare footed persons, two of which foot prints corresponded exactly with the size of the prisoners' feet' and had found sheepskins and the fragment of a shirt believed stolen from the deceased. Hayward then described how he had accompanied Sergeant Major Shaw to search for the murderers, coming upon them 30 or 40 miles from where the murder was committed. Rose then gave his evidence, confirming Hayward's version of events and describing how the latter had measured the feet of the two prisoners.[6] The detail from the evidence given by both Hayward and Rose about Hayward's detective work in measuring the footprints of the alleged murderers is significant.

Magistrate Macdonald did not consider the evidence collected by Hayward and the police sufficient to convict Billy and Jemmy of murder. After the April local court sitting he then wrote a number of letters to the authorities in Adelaide in which he voiced a number of suspicions. He believed that a Yura witness named Peter would greatly assist in the investigation, although his evidence would be hearsay.[7] Obviously fearing for Peter's safety, he advised that a constable should be sent to escort him to Clare if Peter should turn up.[8] Macdonald also reported that one of the two prisoners held in the Redruth gaol had 'volunteered a statement that the murder was committed by his companion'.[9]

Macdonald next reported that he had cancelled the order authorising the discharge of the two suspects because the witness Peter had been found and was being brought to Clare, assuming that the murder trial might proceed.[10] Then in July 1852 Macdonald wrote to the colonial secretary to acquaint executive council with the fact that one of the two suspects had been sent down to Adelaide for trial for murder. Macdonald warned, however, that although he had little doubt that the suspect now in Adelaide Gaol 'is the perpetrator or one of the perpetrators of the murder of Robert Richardson . . . it may be difficult to prove the fact'. Macdonald also advised that the witness Peter had been examined and had provided:

> a reason for the murder on the authority of the prisoner himself, namely that the deceased Richardson had *shot the brother of the prisoner* [Macdonald's emphasis] as well as another native, who, however, recovered. Of these outrages he [Peter] says he was himself an eye-witness.[11]

Macdonald reported that the younger prisoner had been released and had returned to the north under the care of a police constable and that the second suspect, Jemmy, had been sent south to Adelaide for trial. Macdonald made it clear that he feared 'that the settlers might be induced to take the law into their own hands, and that the blacks might be the greater sufferers in the end'.[12] One of the last things we hear of Jemmy on the public record is in the *Register* of 22 November 1852, in which he is named as remanded from August that year because he 'feloniously did kill and murder Robert Richardson, on the 14th of March, 1852, at Youngoona'.

The few remaining official documents about the Richardson murder offer only fragmentary insights into the murder and the events it precipitated. Jemmy was never tried for murder. Hayward refused to travel south to Adelaide to give evidence at his trial. Eventually Jemmy was released and made his way back to the north. The facts about Jemmy's motive for killing Richardson were never revealed. There was no investigation into Hayward's actions in leading a vigilante group against the Yura people he alleged were responsible for Richardson's murder. Hayward was never charged, let alone even named as a murderer. Nevertheless, from records that have survived, official anxiety about the episode is obvious. The upholders of the law were concerned to ensure that justice was seen to be done, perhaps because of an uneasy suspicion that their absence from the district may have precipitated events.

There exists a poignant aftermath to Richardson's murder. In 1853 Patrick James Richardson of Dublin wrote to the colonial secretary in Adelaide inquiring after the whereabouts of his son: a letter sent to his son in South Australia had been returned to Ireland with the word 'Dead' marked on the cover. The police commissioner was asked to deal with Patrick Richardson's request and eventually Fred Hayward was asked by the police to provide details of Richardson's tenure as an employee. Hayward scribbled a note to Corporal Coward that 'there was little or nothing due to him at his death'.[13] It was left to a public servant, B.J. Finnis, to write to Richardson with the official confirmation of his son's death and that there were no wages owing to him.

In June 1852 Protector of Aborigines Dr Matthew Moorhouse submitted his quarterly report to the colonial secretary, and it was published in full in the *Observer*.[14] It is clear that Moorhouse had not visited Aroona to investigate the Richardson murder (he situates Hayward's Run near Lake Torrens), no doubt because he was absent in Victoria on leave to look for gold. Nevertheless, Moorhouse must have spoken with Jemmy, the alleged murderer held in remand in the Adelaide Gaol, in order to ascertain that the suspects' country was Lake Torrens, not the Flinders Ranges.[15]

A month after Richardson's murder, with the Adelaide papers full of news from the Victorian diggings, the northern correspondent of the *Observer* reported that a shepherd had been killed by Yuras at a northern station and a second wounded. 'The fact is, they are *up*, and will not be easily subdued . . . the poor fellow, slain, was buried without an inquest, and *his death was followed by other unavoidable inhumanities* [our emphasis]'.[16] Rumours of massacres were obviously spreading through the north.

A day later the *Register* editorialised about not only the Richardson murder but the wider implications of the withdrawing of police from some of the country stations because of the scarcity of men.[17] As this editorial makes clear, the Mount Remarkable police station was closed on the day of the Richardson murder (14 March 1852) – the station only reopened the day after the Local Court appearance of the two suspects Billy and Jemmy. If Hayward had decided to take the law into his own hands in the weeks after Richardson's murder, there were no police forces stationed in the far north that might have intervened to prevent any bloodshed. Neither was there present a magistrate who might see it as his duty to inform Protector of Aborigines Moorhouse that his services were needed.[18]

There seems to have been no further debate in the Adelaide papers about the Richardson murder and nothing at all was written about the alleged 'collision' it provoked until 50 or more years had passed. It might seem that whatever 'unavoidable inhumanities' had happened at Aroona were destined to fade slowly from the communal memory, only to be revived now and again in diaries and memoirs as a typical example of a number of such violent encounters on the South Australian frontier. But the story of the Richardson murder and its aftermath did not die. In 1928, seventeen years after Johnson Frederick Hayward's death, his son, *Bulletin* journalist C.W.A. Hayward, donated his father's manuscript 'Reminiscences of Johnson Frederick Hayward' to the South Australian Public Library Board for 'preservation in the archives department'.[19] A year later it was published in the 1929 *Proceedings* of the Royal Geographical Society of Australasia (South Australian Branch). From a note in the manuscript held in the Mortlock Library, it seems that it was written in 1871 but remained with the family until its donation.[20]

Hayward's 'Reminiscences' is an historically significant document, a posthumously published foundation memoir. The publication of such memoirs certainly helped confirm the elevation of certain individuals into the pantheon of colonial heroes, but they had a more important cultural function. Such reminiscences began the process of history-making in a culture now ready to see itself as having a past. In the absence of other published histories, foundation memoirs played a central role in offering templates for any future representation of the roaring days. They represented mainstream conservative attitudes based around the cultural supremacy of the pastoral industry in South Australia. Seemingly mundane and plain-speaking memories of the pastoral beginnings of the colony began to take on the aura of romance. Between 1880 and 1930 'the Pastoral Pioneers' were named and valorised, their diaries and reminiscences published, their portraits assembled by the Royal Geographical Society of Australasia (South

Australian Branch). Then their collective histories were published by Rodney Cockburn in the 1920s, first by the *Chronicle* and then later in book form in *The Pastoral Pioneers of South Australia*. Their collective experiences made a history of the far north available to the South Australian public.

Hayward's memoir is typical of a particular kind of posthumously published reminiscence (Alexander Buchanan's is another[21]) in which illegal behaviour – murder – is recorded in substantive detail and with considerable relish. In Hayward's case he hardly bothers to justify his violent actions, stressing as he does his 'hard-won' prosperity. 'The end justifies the means' is the message that comes through most strongly. Neither does he employ the rarely used rhetorical justification that the settlers were at war with Indigenous people, in which event any casualties might be understood as a unfortunate consequences of combat. The Royal Geographical Society of Australasia (South Australian Branch) published Hayward's and Buchanan's memoirs without editorial comment.

It is dangerous to speculate too far about the motives of those who donated such manuscripts or, for that matter, the motives of those who made the decision to publish. It is unlikely, however, that C.W.A. Hayward should have been prompted to open the pages of his father's journal to the world because he felt ashamed of his father's actions, even if the son did work for the *Bulletin*, which by the 1920s still preserved a little of its earlier reputation for radicalism. It is more likely that by the late 1920s it seemed to most Australians that 'the Aboriginal problem' had been solved, just as the social Darwinists of the late nineteenth century had predicted it would be, by the seeming demise of the 'full-blood' Aboriginal population. In the 1870s (when Hayward wrote his memoir) it might have been regretted that criminal behaviour on the frontier had exacerbated the decline of Indigenous Australians. By the late 1920s, with seemingly even fewer living Indigenous Australians, both the scale and the significance of crimes against Indigenous people seemed somehow to have been diminished. Many modern Australians still hold the same beliefs.

The *Advertiser* and the *Register* ran identical articles announcing the donation of the Hayward manuscript in 1928, describing it as 'unusually full and vividly descriptive of early pastoral life in South Australia'.[22] Both articles contained hagiographic commentary on Hayward's reminiscences. 'They are the work of a fine type of English gentleman, with no narrow or selfish view of a native problem, which was to him, a vital one; a man of generous, kindly instincts, determination and boundless courage'.[23] Yet most readers today would note that Hayward's memoir stresses the leading role he took in organising not one but a number of campaigns against the Yura.[24] At one point Hayward writes that 'had I kept a diary in those days it must have repeated itself every weak [sic] in "Visits to flocks and stations" and "Occasional hunts after niggers".[25] His choice of the noun 'hunts' is telling, employing as it does the characteristic colonial trope in which Indigenous people are represented as 'fair game'.

Hayward's 'Reminiscences' details a remarkable level of conflict between the squatters and the Yura people. From the evidence of his own pen, 'pursuits' were numerous on both Pekina and Aroona, the two far north runs he managed. He describes flogging a Yura sheepstealer with a stockwhip after sentence had been passed by a 'drum-head court martial'.[26] He reveals that at least one member of the legal profession, a magistrate named Pang, had cause to reflect on Hayward's growing political influence.[27] His employers were, variously, Price Maurice on Pekina and then later on Aroona the brothers Drs W. J. and J. Harris Browne, among the richest and most powerful men in the South Australian colony in the 1850s. In 1864 Hayward married the second daughter of Captain C.W. Litchfield, Chief Inspector of Police in South Australia.[28]

On his own admission Hayward was determined to punish Yura sheepstealers and he was prepared to use his employers' political influence to ensure he got his way. His contempt for the law whenever an individual lacking 'colonial experience' did his best to uphold it is also clearly revealed.[29] He makes it clear that he fired on the Yura on more than one occasion, in that he describes the men of the Yura group making their escape by carrying children, knowing that, in Hayward's own words, he and his men 'never fired on such or women'.[30]

The Richardson murder and the 'campaign' against the Yura which it provoked is described by Hayward in great detail. The names of the Europeans involved are freely given. No other reminiscence published in South Australia is quite so forthcoming about such a violent 'collision' on the frontier. The detail is such as to suggest that Hayward may well have kept a journal that enabled him to reconstruct events 20 years later.

Hayward describes hearing of Richardson's murder, viewing the corpse, measuring the tracks of the suspects and determining through 'native rumour' who they might be. He then insists that his men were in a state of consternation about the murder, unwilling to perform their duties, prompting him to take decisive action. On hearing that 'the aborigines were mustering from all quarters, intending a raid on my homestead, and breathing out threatenings and slaughter against me and my sheep', Hayward decided to take the law into his own hands. He found some support for his proposed action at his neighbour Septimus Boord's run at Oraparinna, but H.S. Price at Wilpena refused to allow his men to participate in any vigilante action. Hayward then ascertained where the Yuras were camped, in a gorge between the Heysen and the ABC ranges, about four miles from Youngoona and thirteen miles south of Aroona homestead. With several companions (all of whom are named) Hayward and his men made their way at night to the Yura camp, 'determined to attack them at dawn' and capture the males, among them those suspected of Richardson's murder.

There was shooting. Hayward describes 'a good fusillade' on the Yura camp. He does not attempt to quantify the number of casualties beyond recording 'probably the wounding of a few'. He insists that most of the Yuras escaped during the attack.[31] However, he admits that word rapidly spread through the Flinders Ranges and beyond that there had been a significant number of casualties, as the *Observer* news item suggests.[32] In the final published version of his account of the episode, Hayward claims that 'they reported at Wilpena and other stations that we had killed fifteen blackfellows'. In the 1871 Mortlock manuscript in Hayward's own hand, the original wording is '. . . that we had killed 40, 50 or 60 blackfellows', with '40, 50 or 60' lined through and '15 or 20' written in above.[33] Between 1852 and 1929 a downward revision in the speculations or rumours about the numbers of casualties is clearly evident – a rewriting evident not only in the two versions of the Hayward text but also manifest in the decision taken by editor of the *Proceedings* of the Royal Geographical Society of Australasia (South Australian Branch) to print 'fifteen' without comment.

The vigilante raid was not successful in capturing the suspects for Richardson's murder. It was later when the police eventually arrived at Aroona that Billy and Jemmy were arrested and taken south in custody. Hayward's expressed reluctance to travel to the Clare court to testify against them is revealing, given his earlier insistence in the memoir that he 'never thought of distances, or loss of time, or fatigue, in any case that deserved punishment'.[34] Initially he seemed determined to accompany the prisoners south to the Clare lock-up, 250 miles away, but then obviously he felt some reluctance to leave Aroona with the police party and the prisoners – many of the hands had left the employ of the squatters for the Victorian diggings. By this stage, of course, the police were involved and 'a drum-head court martial'[35] was out of the question. Perhaps Hayward had in mind the furore both in South Australia and back in Britain caused by O'Halloran's drum-head court martial and execution of two Milmenrura suspects for the murders of the survivors of the *Maria* a dozen years before. Whatever his thinking, Hayward notes that he 'could not escape prosecuting, and the police sergeant insisted, only stopping short of compulsion',[36] an eloquent observation, strongly suggesting that British justice was determined to bring the case to court.[37]

Hayward never managed (and was never compelled) to attend court, either as a witness in Clare or later in the Supreme Court in Adelaide. Peter the interpreter had disappeared – a fortunate turn for Hayward, one suspects – and the two arrested men languished in gaol for far longer than they should have been held before being brought to trial. Hayward also makes reference to the (unnamed) Protector of Aborigines: Moorhouse was on leave in Victoria when Richardson was killed and unable to investigate the murder until his return. Hayward was in the clear.

As a footnote to his descriptions of the Richardson murder, the arrest of the two suspects and their eventual release because the case did not come to trial, Hayward leaves a telling detail for last. When Billy and Jemmy were eventually released and returned to their country, they 'speedily received from some unknown hand the penalty due to their misdeeds'.[38] Perhaps the payback killings of Billy and Jemmy came from the hand of 'Big' John McKinlay[39] or one of his employees. Later to become famous as a tough and uncompromising explorer, McKinlay had 'bush experience' gained from squatting on the Darling and was, it seems, no stranger to violence on the frontier. He was also a friend of Hayward.[40] It seems that the settlers in the Flinders were well able to practise the behaviour commonly attributed to 'savage' or 'primitive' Indigenous Australians: payback. John Bowyer Bull notes in a contemporary diary entry when speaking of Aboriginal practice that 'there [*sic*] law is man for man'[41] but he might as well have been speaking of his compatriots.

Bull[42] has left an intriguing comment or two about Hayward and the events on Aroona. Bull worked for various leaseholders in several parts of South Australia and his 'Reminiscences' provide a unique and detailed insight into the everyday detail of pastoral life in the 1850s and 1860s. In 1855 he took up a job with John Chambers on his Bobmoonie (Bob Mooney) West run, north of Oratunga and east of Beltana. Bull's first job for Chambers was to drive 7000 sheep from the latter's Minbrie Run near Franklin Harbour on Eyre Peninsula to Bobmoonie, riding north past Aroona to reach his destination. His handwritten diary entry describes the trip as follows:

> I did not see my Black friends on the road back, & was rather glad, after I heard the way other whites had been treeting them, and knowing there law is man for man, of course they look on the white man as there jeneral enemy, taking there waters and hunting grounds from them and giving them no recompence for it, but shooting them down, so what do they care who the white man is as long as they see a easy chance for revenge. . . . On my road up to my destenation, at Wolpena & Arrona Stations, I saw nothing but Black wommen in the camps, I asked the reason & they told me whitefellows shootem alabout Blackfellow.[43]

Bull is describing Aroona in August 1855, over three years after the Richardson murder and the ensuing 'campaign'. His discovery on the road up to Aroona and Wilpena of Yura camps without men can be interpreted two ways. First, Bull's words clearly suggest that Hayward's representation of the campaign as achieving little more than frightening a few Yuras can be challenged. Second, he records an Indigenous storytelling tradition of anecdotes about the killing of Yura people in the Flinders Ranges.

John Bowyer Bull's diaries were certainly known to his father, John Wrathall Bull,[44] whose *Early Experiences of Life in South Australia* gives a brief account of Richardson's murder and a 'fight' between Hayward, his neighbours and 'the natives' that 'resulted in the death of several of the blacks'.[45] There are some intriguing details in Bull senior's version – he insists that not one but *two* shepherds were murdered, that Hayward organised and led the reprisals, that several 'blacks' were killed in the 'fight' between settlers and Yuras and large numbers of sheep were recovered.

A third (more-or-less) contemporaneous account of what had happened at Aroona can be found in another unpublished handwritten manuscript in the Mortlock Library, 'Reminiscences Past to Present by Richard Dewdney';[46] possibly written by him in 1924 in the year of his death. Dewdney's version of the story of the Aroona killings is obviously based on what he had heard from some of the participants (no doubt from the Marchant brothers, leaseholders of the Arkaba and Wilpena runs) almost a decade after the events had occurred. It seems that the stories Dewdney heard about the early 1850s may have reversed the order of events (in so far as it can be determined about what might have happened). Dewdney reports a siege of the Aroona headstation, whereas Hayward in his memoir records that he and his band of vigilantes acted to *prevent* an attack on Aroona. Dewdney's account of Aroona in the 1850s begins with his description of a tiff between the squatters Septimus Boord of Oraparinna and Fred Hayward of Aroona – their leases shared boundaries. Dewdney writes as follows:

> Blacks at that time were & had been giving much trouble, to such an extent as to inforce use of Fire Arms. Septimus had been South, and had just arrived at Wilpena from Port Augusta with Bullock teams with rations ([they had?] their own teamsters in those days). On arrival at Wilpena, [he] heard the news, Aroona stuck up and surrounded with Blacks, Huts only of pine and thatched roofs, barracaded with Station hands unable to get out, and sadly in need of assistance. No police in those days, nor were they sought for. Septimus, however, on hearing the news, turned out his bullocks and collecting what men and instruments of protection or Slaughter, made a B line for Aroona. Result a speedy retreat of the Blacks. History in those days did not record casualties, any way trouble ended [illegible]. [Hayward and Boord] met, shook hands, Sep. remarking now you are free, you can. . . . [illegible]. But Fred, viewing the matter in an Englishman's light, and for all time there after they remained friends. No doubt younger men remain [illegible] on hearing of these occasional outbreaks with the Blacks. Following that just related, a shepherd at the Youngoona outstation of Aroona had been murdered. The Blacks per force taking refuge in what then as now known as ABC Ranges south of St Mary's Peak. It was here during [illegible] the said Johnny Bose [illegible] an Aroona stockman, would have if at home caught, got into trouble for shooting an impudent Black, but then in his wisdom kept out of the way until matters quietened.[47]

The evidence is fragmentary. Nevertheless, Dewdney records a version of the oral history of the 1852 encounter that contains some details of the 'troubles' or 'outbreaks' between settlers and the Yura, stressing that such episodes were usually solved with firearms. He records a barricading of Hayward's Aroona homestead, relieved only by Septimus Boord's intervention with his men from Oraparinna, the neighbouring run. He insists that there was shooting, but does not give casualty figures. He mentions both Richardson's murder (which he claims was subsequent to the Aroona siege) and an expedition against the Yura somewhere in the ABC Range. Whatever the historical veracity of his version, Dewdney records in fragmentary form the bare bones of the story, deploying the level of detail characteristic of everyday yarning about a violent past that might have been heard in the far north a century ago. Dewdney's reminiscence reveals that stories were told about Hayward's infamous tenure on Aroona. The 1925 *Advertiser* obituary for Hayward's widow describes Aroona as being 'famous for a memorable fight with the blacks in 1852'.[48] Interestingly, Hayward's own obituary does not mention any such episode.[49]

There are at least two more texts in which Fred Hayward and the Richardson murder are represented, both written by Robert Bruce. Bruce migrated to South Australia in 1854 and worked in Customs and Excise at Port Adelaide until, it appears, he had to resign in disgrace for 'gross irregularities'.[50] In 1858 he decided to join his brother Douglas, who was working as an overseer for Fred Hayward on Aroona. Douglas had intended that Robert join him in Hayward's employ but, as it turned out, Robert took a job with Frank Marchant on the Arkaba Run just to the south of Wilpena Pound. He stayed there for two years before eventually taking up the Wallerberdina Run to the west, where he remained until 1860 before taking up the Coondambo Run northwest of Port Augusta between Woomera and Kingoonya.

In the 1890s, in his sixties and in semi-retirement, Bruce wrote a novel, *Benbonuna*, and a memoir, *Reminiscences of an Old Squatter*, writing not about his decades on Coondambo out on the plains, but about his two years as a young man on the Arkaba Run in the Flinders. In his *Reminiscences of an Old Squatter*, Bruce describes his first meeting with Fred Hayward, or 'Mr H.' as he is named, mentioning in passing his reputation with the Yura:

In the natives' estimation, Mr H was a great man, for, though he treated them with uniform kindness, he was not to be trifled with, as they found when they murdered one of his shepherds, stole a number of his sheep, and were then settled up with.[51]

Bruce makes a further remarkable observation about Hayward in his *Reminiscences of an Old Squatter*. When describing a second visit to Aroona, Bruce remembers a certain practical joke. He and Frank Marchant decided to capture and restrain a number of the younger stockmen about the run and give them 'a little artistic pruning of the whiskers'.[52] Bruce has this to say about the joke:

At any rate, that shaving racket was a merrie conceit at which all parties concerned have laughed many a time since. I may say that we left Mr H and my brother severely alone, they carried too many guns for us.[53]

Hayward was obviously a man not to be trifled with, even a man to be feared, especially when armed with two of Mr Colt's revolvers, which he mentions had cost him £23 in Adelaide in February 1853. The Yura had even more cause to fear this man who seems to have made even a fellow-squatter think twice about involving him in simple horseplay.[54]

Bruce specifically refers to the Richardson murder and its aftermath in his memoir. Between 1858 and 1860 Bruce made at least two trips from Arkaba to Aroona to see his brother. He describes riding southeast with Douglas from Aroona towards Oraparinna to the hut where Richardson had been murdered,[55] noting that 'a few neighbouring settlers ran their tracks and taught them such a lesson that in future a shepherd or stockman was safe on any of the runs in the vicinity' and that the hut was named after the Lake Hope cockatoo Younganna.[56] Bruce gets the date wrong (Richardson's murder occurred in 1852, not 1855) and controversially insists that the shepherd had his caul (or kidney) fat removed, an assertion for which there is no evidence. There are, incidentally, occasional references to this (alleged) practice in many colonial memoirs like Bruce's, where such behaviour (like cannibalism and infanticide) is offered as a measure of Indigenous savagery and barbarism.

Bruce's assertion that the (un-named) settlers *tracked down* the perpetrators of the murder is significant. Hayward is not named as one of the 'trackers', but Bruce's choice of the verb is revealing, given that the evidence against the suspects arrested for Richardson's murder was the measurement of their footprints collected by Hayward at the scene.

The Richardson murder and its aftermath also indirectly shaped the plot of Bruce's *Benbonuna*, a popular novel first serialised in Adelaide and Port Augusta papers in the late 1890s, published in book-length form first in Adelaide in 1900 and later reprinted in 1904 in London in Long's Colonial Library series. A reading of *Benbonuna* reveals how it contributes to the habit of silence about violence on the South Australian frontier in avoiding any overt representation of armed conflict between the squatters and the Yura. In deciding to rework his subject – pastoral experience in the Flinders Range in the 1850s – according to what he understood as the conventions of the Rolf Boldrewood-inspired bush romance, Bruce played his part in the creation and maintenance of a preferred version of the 'history' of European occupation and settlement that idealised the squatters and marginalised the Yura and their attempts to resist the invaders.

The squatter-detective who solves the mystery in the novel, Tom Bowyer, is clearly based on Fred Hayward. In a biographical note published in 1927 in *Pastoral Pioneers of South Australia*, Rodney Cockburn writes that 'although the story does not say so, the scene of it *[Benbonuna]* was laid at the old Arkaba Station, and some of the characters were actually true to life'.[57] This remark suggests that as late as the 1920s readers of the novel with personal knowledge of Hayward and his activities in the Flinders would have made the connection.

Bruce represents Bowyer as a detective who solves a murder mystery because he can measure tracks in the sand. Bruce transforms Hayward from murderer to hero. No doubt those in the know smiled knowingly about the transformation, enjoying the insider's recognition of a sanitised version of history in the making, a history that eulogises the squatter and erases any reference to Indigenous resistance.

Why did Bruce not write a novel in which he fictionalised the Richardson murder and the 'campaign' against the Yura that it provoked? Why did he rework history? Why did he prefer 'King Romance' to Mr Colt's revolver-shots of unparleying fact, to adapt Joseph Furphy's remarks in his own essay on romance in his 1901 novel *Such is Life*? *Benbonuna* can be read as an assertion of prevailing ideologies that find their overt expression in the popular fictions of the time. Instead of representing a stern, humourless, uncompromising, gun-toting pastoralist like Hayward, Bruce's memories of his brother's employer are transformed utterly by the demands of romance fiction in the Rolf Boldrewood manner. In the novel, Hayward becomes the skilled bushman Tom Bowyer, a cheerful giant, an egalitarian, well-read and perceptive individual with a great set of teeth: the archetypal squatter. There are no murderous campaigns against the Yura in *Benbonuna* but instead a sunny world in which at least some of the surviving Yura are depicted as skilled and lively, if marginalised, participants in the pastoral enterprise and where all the villains are ex-convicts and bushrangers.

Bruce's *Benbonuna* suggests that by 1900 there was a general reluctance in South Australia to speak too loudly about violence on the frontier in the early days of settlement. Just seven years before the publication of *Benbonuna*, Simpson Newland, another South Australian 'old squatter' and distinguished politician and public figure, published the much better-known novel *Paving the Way*. Like *Benbonuna*, *Paving the Way* is a curious and ambivalent blending of romance and realism. Unlike Bruce, Simpson Newland represents in fictional form many of the affrays that actually took place between settlers and Indigenous South Australians. Events represented in his novel took place between about 1839 and 1850 along the Coorong, in the Rufus River area, in the Tatiara and on the Darling River in western New South Wales. In spite of his obvious interest in history, Simpson Newland still has this to say in his preface:

> As, in a work on Australian pioneer life such as this purports to be, it might be difficult to present bare facts in an acceptable form to the general public, my object has been to blend truth and fiction in a connected narrative. That it partakes largely of a romance is certain, but the incidents, though so romantic, are mainly authentic; for these lives have been lived and these deaths have been died. It is not alone on the familiar ground of the Old World that heroic deeds have been performed or suffering nobly endured.
>
> To particularise too closely would not add interest to the story for the public, though it might in the opinion of those acquainted with many of the occurrences alluded to or more or less related. I have endeavoured to wound as few susceptibilities and tread on as few toes as possible; the time has not yet arrived in the life of Australia when the historian or novelist can write with an untrammelled pen.[58]

One of the powerful forces that affected the turn-of-the-century writer's freedom to explore the darker moments of the frontier past was the dominance of romance conventions. There seems to have been a general feeling that stories of violence on the frontier might only be hinted at or treated obliquely – if they were to be mentioned at all – as typical of the kinds of threats to the pastoral enterprise posed by dingoes, drought or bushfire. This complex mediation contributed to the characteristic silence about the 'dark side' of the Australian foundation story.

You might think that by the turn of the century there would have been few rich and respectable pillars of society – men like Hayward – who were keen on having their sordid, violent and illegal activities on the frontier scrutinised in historical writing for the public record. However, a surprising number wrote revealing memoirs that were published (sometimes posthumously) by reputable institutions such as the Royal Geographical Society of Australasia or publishing houses attached to the major newspapers in Adelaide, many of them in the 1920s. While Hayward may have been honest about his behaviour in a diary written for his family, in transforming his recollections of his brother's employer, Bruce demonstrates a more typical attitude to memories of frontier violence. Nothing can be gained by resurrecting memories of murder, his novel suggests. This country needed men like Hayward before it could be 'opened up'. If there were a few casualties here and there, they died for the greater good, paving the way for those of us who follow. Prime Minister Howard would no doubt celebrate Robert Bruce's erasures, his tact, his reluctance to dwell on the sordid details of frontier violence.

The example of *Benbonuna* suggests that by the 1890s Robert Bruce was more concerned to see his name on the cover of a novel in Long's Colonial Library than to attempt an historical study based on what he must have known of Hayward's 'campaigns' against the Yura in the 1850s. It seems that in 1900 it was still too early to 'write with an untrammelled pen'. While Chinese whispers about heads in camp ovens and massacres were circulating on South Australia's west coast, while stories about arsenic poisonings and heroic rides were being told about the Tatiara, one story about a massacre in the Flinders was erased through its transformation into a ripping yarn.

Have things changed? In 1996 Sue Barker, Murray McCaskill and Brian Ward published their splendidly produced, information-packed and copiously illustrated guidebook *Explore the Flinders Ranges* for the Royal Geographical Society of Australasia (South Australian Branch). The book reflects the contemporary interest in repackaging impressions of country like the Flinders for the rapidly expanding eco- and cultural tourism markets (although there is much more information available about the former rather than the latter). The contributors' list takes up a full page and reflects a distinguished and comprehensive cross-section of mostly South Australian friends of the Flinders: several members of the Yura community, the Indigenous owners of the Flinders; a number of South Australian government departments; university departments, private organisations and other instrumentalities.[59]

Explore the Flinders Ranges[60] contains the following brief history of pastoral activity in the Flinders in the 1850s and 1860s. It is clear that the writers have J.F. Hayward's[61] regime on Aroona in mind:

> As part of this settlement process the Aboriginal people of the Ranges had been thoroughly subdued and virtually displaced from occupation of their traditional lands. The survivors of this one-sided conflict had little choice but to come to terms with the loss of their land and most drifted on to stations, government ration depots and missions from where they provided cheap labour to the pastoral industry for over a century.
>
> In the early years shepherds, hut keepers and some of the pastoralists themselves were guilty of appalling cruelty and murder. Hans Mincham documents much of this in *The Story of the Flinders Ranges*, including cases of stock camps and stations having only Aboriginal women present, the men having been shot. Considering the attitudes of the time and the fact that many of the itinerant bush workers were former convicts from the eastern states, such cruelty is perhaps not surprising. Similar excesses have been documented throughout Australia.[62]

Old myths die hard in South Australia. Hayward's direct, personal involvement in the conflict with the Yura people is not mentioned. Some un-named pastoralists are accused of appalling cruelty and murder, but it is their employees, their shepherds and hut keepers whom readers are invited to blame first. The records certainly reveal that some of those shepherds and hut keepers were ex-convicts and there is evidence that in South Australia a (small?) number of ex-convicts from the colonies of the eastern seaboard were 'guilty of appalling cruelty and

murder'. There were no convicts in South Australia, goes the argument, therefore the levels of violence were not as great as in New
South Wales or Queensland. If there is to be any blame apportioned
for violence on the frontier, then better lay fault at the feet of old lags,
of 'Vandemenians'. South Australians still like to think that in this
colony 'the Aboriginal problem' was handled with greater tolerance and
sensitivity and led to lower levels of frontier violence than elsewhere
in Australia.

Explore the Flinders Ranges has little to say about Hayward's time
on Aroona (save for the fact that he sold the Aroona run for £40 000)
and nothing about an (alleged) massacre in the ABC Range in which
he played a leading role. The title of the book suits contemporary attitudes to places like the Flinders: in suggesting that this landscape is
available for those adventurers who wish to 'explore', there is just a
hint of the commonly held view that many contemporary Australian
landscapes are 'wilderness'. Visitors driving through in their 4WDs or
on their bus tours like to think that these benign and photogenic landscapes are (more or less) pristine: who has ever told them that once they
were fought over? The existing material evidence of the 'golden age'
of pastoral activity can still be found here and there by the explorer,
but as time passes such evidence seems almost as fleeting and transient
as the surviving signs of the traditional culture of the Aboriginal
inhabitants. What seems permanent in the Flinders landscapes are
not the fading signs of human activity but those iconic vistas that we
now think represent the country more meaningfully, like 'The Spirit of
Endurance', the redgum to the north of Wilpena Pound photographed
by Harold Cazneaux in 1937.

Such attitudes to *some* landscapes are deeply entrenched in contemporary Australian culture.[63] What we see still partially reflected in the
1996 publication *Explore the Flinders Ranges* is on-going evidence of
Stanner's 'Great Australian Silence', the admittedly ambivalent maintenance of the 'pioneer legend' that has led to the *partial* erasure of
Indigenous history from the public memory. No pamphlet has been
produced that might encourage bushwalkers in the National Park to
walk into the site of the 'affray' between squatters, their employees and
the Yura in rough country between the ABC and the Heysen Ranges,
a place where visitors could reflect on the brutal history of dispossess-
sion.[64] Instead the visitor will find the following sign at the ruins of
Youngoona Hut:

One of a number of outstation huts established on reliable waters by Frederick Haywood in 1852 from his head station at Aroona.

Shepherds were employed to tend sheep flocks before the introduction of fencing – sheep were generally yarded at night to protect them from attacks by dingoes.

Huts were built entirely of local materials, mud mortared stone chimneys and mud sealed vertical pine walls were weather proofed with 'whitewash', roofs were thatched with reeds and grasses, floors formed from rammed earth or flagstones.

The implication of the sign is Youngoona Hut and the memories of its history are as fragile and transitory as the materials from which the hut was once constructed. All that is left now is part of the stone chimney: in time it too will fall back to the earth. The memories of Richardson's murder and its violent aftermath are just as transitory.

In 1996 South Australian writer Ann Clancy published the novel *The Wild Colonial Girl*,[65] another fictional foray into Hayward's tenure on Aroona. The novel details cruelty and murder on the frontier in the Flinders, suggesting that often the violence between the settlers and the Yura was exacerbated by the absence of European women.[66] Clancy draws comparisons between the behaviour of English landlords, violence and evictions in Ireland and the treatment of Indigenous people in Australia. She mentions that the settlers poisoned the Yura, eradicating them as if they were pests like the dingo.[67] She refers to the shooting of woman and children in retaliation for sheep stealing, to the 'silent war that raged throughout the far North'.[68] Her heroine Kate O'Mara intervenes and prevents a massacre by shooting the overseer Angus Campbell. Although Clancy acknowledges her use of J.F. Hayward's diary in researching *The Wild Colonial Girl*, she does not make extensive use of his version of what happened after the murder of Robert Richardson. She represents James Carmichael as the initiator of the massacre, in that he orders his overseer Campbell to track down and kill the ringleaders of the Yura suspected of sheep-stealing. Like Tom Bowyer, Carmichael is a fictional reworking of Fred Hayward, but in *The Wild Colonial Girl* he does not retire a wealthy man but instead is crippled, doomed to play a gloomy Rochester to O'Mara's Jane Eyre. Carmichael is as highly mediated by modern romance conventions as was Bruce's portrait of Tom Bowyer written almost a century before. Nevertheless, it says a great deal about the so-called 'women's romance writing' of our time that Clancy should have made creative use of some aspects of Fred Hayward's 'Reminiscences'. But on balance, Simpson Newland's words still seem appropriate: the time has still not arrived when the novelist can write with an untrammelled pen.

LOGIC'S UNEXPECTED
CELEBRITY

∎

In April 1878 Adelaide newspapers reported that Cornelius Mulholland, a stockman, had been murdered by Aborigines in the far north-east of South Australia. The news was conveyed by David Walker who, like Mulholland, was employed by William Burkett on his newly established Tinga Tingana Run at the southern end of Strzelecki Creek. By his own account, Walker was lucky to be alive, claiming that 'had it not been for his fleet horse he would have met the same fate, as his horse was struck by a boomerang'.[1] While early reports gave no reason for the attack, it was suggested that the removal of police from the Mount Freeling station had made the Aborigines 'bolder' and the country 'more dangerous to travel through'.[2] The murder became secondary to a general discussion about the role of police in outlying districts and would probably have remained just another vague account of frontier violence had it not been for a letter published in the *Adelaide Observer* a few weeks later in which the events surrounding the murder were detailed.

The letter was written by Nathaniel Phillipson, a station manager on a run that adjoined Tinga Tingana, and was addressed to his friend and business partner, Peter Waite. Commenting on an earlier letter in which a correspondent calling himself 'Humanity' described a state of violence existing in the district, he wrote:

> 'Humanity' and his informant, David Walker, have given themselves entirely up to fiction without having the least regard for fact, and as you and I have often discussed the matter of the most advisable plan of bringing blacks to justice for misdemeanours, I think in justice to our black brethren I ought to submit the

following information in reference to their conduct for some time past . . .[3]

According to Phillipson, David Walker was not with the stockman when he was killed and consequently could hardly have ridden off evading boomerangs. Far from being murdered by 'the natives', the stockman was killed by his Aboriginal assistant. Phillipson also contradicted Walker's claim that 'the natives along Strzelecki Creek are hostile'; writing instead that they had 'not been the least trouble for some years past in the neighbourhood of Cooper's Creek and Streletzki Creek'.[4] He characterised the reports of the murder as 'extraordinary and fictitious statements'. The early reports were wrong on another point: the victim's name was Cornelius Mulhall – not Mulholland.[5]

Phillipson went on to say that Mulhall and his Aboriginal 'horseboy', Logic, had been out four days, riding the southern boundary of the station in search of cattle, when an argument erupted. Mulhall complained that Logic was not keeping up and struck him with his stockwhip and, a short time later, 'on the black becoming insolent shot him in the lower part of the back'.[6] By this time camp had been established near a claypan and at sunset Logic tried to get on his horse and ride back to the station, but he was prevented from doing so and given another flogging for his trouble.[7] The dispute escalated when Logic refused an order to fetch some wood and, instead, went to a claypan to wash the clotted blood from his wounds. Mulhall followed and a fight began when Logic was once more stockwhipped for his insubordination. During the struggle, Logic got Mulhall 'in a tight grip around the neck while with the other [hand] he took a pocket knife out of Mulholland's trouser pocket, which he opened with his teeth and stabbed him in the temple, and then stabbed him all over the head and chest'.[8] He finished the job by smashing his skull with a stick. Badly wounded, Logic secretly returned to the homestead, where he related his version of events to a friend at the station before slipping off into the bush.[9]

George, the Aboriginal man whom Logic had confided in before clearing out, led a search party to the corpse, and it was through him that the details of the fatal encounter became known. Thomas Bollard, the manager of Tinga Tingana station, and Edward Long, overseer of an adjoining station, accompanied George to the murder site and their observations supported George's story. Evidence of the struggle was imprinted in the now dry and crusted surface of the claypan. They found the stockwhip and, nearby, Logic's trousers clotted in blood. There was a bullet hole in the back of the trousers but none at the front, suggesting that the bullet was still in his thigh. Besides getting an account of the events from Thomas Bollard, Phillipson wrote, he also spoke to George, who related Logic's version.[10]

For such an account, so damning of a fellow settler, to become public was exceedingly rare. In this period cases of mistreatment rarely reached the courts and when they did they were not often successful as the settlers would rarely testify against 'their own' and Aboriginal evidence was given little weight.

Soon after the report of the murder, Police Commissioner Hamilton ordered Sergeant O'Shanahan, three police troopers and an Aboriginal tracker to search for Logic. The search continued for several months, but was given up in July 1878 when it was reported that Logic had crossed the Great Stoney Desert into Queensland.[11]

Sometime in late September or early October 1880 Logic returned to the area of Strzelecki Creek, where he was recognised by locals and held on Tinga Tingana Station until police arrived.[12] They arrested him on 2 November 1880.[13] Logic and three witnesses in the case were escorted south by Mounted Constable Power, arriving in Adelaide in mid-December. The trial was heard in the Supreme Court on 22 February 1881 before Justice James Penn Boucaut.[14] Logic pleaded 'not guilty of feloniously and of malice aforethought murdering Cornelius Mulhall on March 25, 1878'.[15] Prosecuting the case for the crown was Richard Andrews, a man of considerable experience, having been crown solicitor and public prosecutor since 1870.[16] Of Logic's lawyer, John Nicholson, very little is known, beyond the fact that he had only recently been admitted to the South Australian bar, having moved from Queensland.[17]

The first witness called in the trial was Thomas Bollard, manager of Tinga Tingana Station at the time of the murder and the man in charge of the search party that recovered the stockman's body.[18] According to Bollard's testimony, Mulhall and Logic had been instructed to ride the outside boundary and check on the cattle, a task that he judged would take four or five days given the inclement weather at that time. Bollard's suspicions were raised when the Aboriginal people on the station deserted their usual camp about two days after the pair had set out. Logic had returned in the night and related his story to those in the camp, before he, and the others, fled. Hearing the story from George, who had remained behind, Bollard was convinced that Mulhall had been killed and organised a search party.

They followed the group's tracks for about 65 kilometres until they came upon a deserted camp where Logic's boots were recovered. The party found no sign of Logic but they did apprehend two Aboriginal women and one man. At this point, perhaps after questioning the trio, they gave up their pursuit of Logic and instead concentrated on recovering Mulhall's body, which they found 40 kilometres south of the station. Bollard said that Mulhall's revolver, which he usually carried in a pouch on his belt, was found in the seat of his pants. The knife and two sticks that had been used to kill him were found nearby.[19] It was established that the knife belonged to Logic, as a bushman on the station had given it to him.

The tracker George was the next to give evidence. After outlining George's part in the events, prosecutor Andrews drew the witness out on a conversation between Charley, an Aboriginal worker on the station, and Logic that allegedly took place the night Logic secretly returned to the station. George had heard Charley and Logic. Charley, he said, had asked Logic how he had killed the 'whitefellow', and Logic had said 'he killed him with his waddy then he killed him with his knife'.[20] The crown's final witness was Charley, who said:

> I had a jabber with Logic – George was there. Logic said that Con kept telling him to come on and then hit him with a stock whip. Logic said that he replied, 'If you hit 'em me, me killem you' and when they went to sit down Logic killed him.[21]

The strategy of the defence was to show that Logic's actions had been provoked by Mulhall's ill-treatment. In his cross-examination of both George and Charley, he showed that Logic had been both stockwhipped and shot before the fatal encounter.[22] Nicholson also attempted to show that Logic was not prone to violence and that his actions in this instance were out of character. European station workers Bollard and Robinson testified that Logic was generally 'good tempered', the former adding that he 'never heard complaints about him'. A final witness, Harrold Sparkes, who had worked with Logic for four months in Queensland, reported that he 'never showed any temper or malice and very good lad indeed'.[23] With this mitigating evidence in mind the jury found Logic not guilty of the charge of murder, but guilty of manslaughter. He was sentenced to 14 years' hard labour.[24]

Logic became prisoner No. 2020 at Adelaide's Yatala Labour Prison in late February 1880.[25] According to the prisoner's register, Logic was about 24 years of age and married with two children. He is described as five feet six sixes in height and eleven stone seven ounces – in other words, short and somewhat stocky in build. His occupation is listed as stockrider and his religion as 'Heathen'.[26]

Logic probably spent much of his time working in the quarries that adjoined the prison. Each morning at six the work gangs were assembled in the prison compound and marched, in chains, to one of the prison's five quarries. Many, notably the long-termers, worked in leg-irons, and were kept apart from the short-term prisoners. Two hours a day were allowed for meals and two spells were permitted for smoking. Rain, which made the quarries slippery and dangerous, was one of the few things that brought the quarrying to a stop. Guard boxes were placed strategically throughout the quarries so warders could keep an eye on the prisoners. The long day ended at six o'clock, when the prisoners were again assembled and marched back to their cells.[27]

The superintendent of Yatala during the period of Logic's incarceration was Edward Bates Scott. He was a friend of the explorer Edward Eyre and accompanied him on some of his expeditions. Scott also joined Eyre on the Murray River when Eyre was appointed Sub-protector of Aborigines, a position Scott took over a few years after Eyre's departure. Superintendent Scott's official journal indicates that life was more than usually difficult in this period as Yatala was greatly overcrowded. There were consistently more than 250 prisoners accommodated in the prison between the years 1880 and 1886.[28] In January 1882 Scott recorded in his journal that 'there are now 51 Prisoners without cell accommodation & this undesirable state of things has been going on for two years & more'.[29] If anything the situation became worse in following years. Perhaps desperation born of poverty contributed to the overcrowding of the prison. The colony was entering a recession and thousands of people, many fresh from the immigration depot, were out of work and living on the streets.

In early October 1885 Logic petitioned the colony's Governor, William Cleaver Robinson, for a remission of his sentence. The petition summarised Logic's conduct in Yatala and his hope for the future:

> your Petitioner has now been incarcerated four years and eight months (4yrs – 8 mo.) during which time he has never committed

a single breach of the Rules of the Prison. That he has worked hard and well. That he is totally ignorant being unable to read or write. That upon being released your Petitioner would gladly return to his own country & earn an honest living.[30]

The petition, which had a good chance of success, was duly channelled through the bureaucracy. Scott signed and dated it before sending it on to a medical officer, who noted Logic's state of health. The colonial secretary was next to receive it and he handed it over to Governor Robinson's under-secretary. The petition was virtually in the governor's hands when Logic escaped from Yatala.

On the afternoon of 15 October Logic was a member of a work gang in Quarry No. 1. It seems that the last task of the day was to blast rock so that it would be ready to work with pick and shovel first thing next morning. Prison-guard Barrien issued instructions to prisoners Makius and Logic to light the fuses and then run back to the others who were waiting some distance away, ready to be marched back to the prison. While this was happening, another prison-guard, Bolger, was supposed to be on post duty, keeping an eye on the prisoners as they carried out their task. No one, it seems, had told Bolger that blasting was about to take place.[31]

Thinking that the day's work was over, Bolger wandered into Quarry No. 1 just as the shout 'Fire!' went up. In imminent danger of being buried under potential road metal and building stone, he fled for the cover of a nearby watershed. After the shots had been fired and the dust was settling Bolger came out of the shed and, as he later reported, 'saw one prisoner join the gang and concluded that the other joined at the same time'.[32] The other guard, Barrien, from his position with the waiting work gang, described the event somewhat differently:

> I moved on with the gang out of the way of the blasts and the two men should have followed after lighting the fuse, but only one overtook me (Prisoner Makius). I thought an accident had happened to the other man (Prisoner Logic).[33]

Barrien reported that he was ordered back to the quarry, where he met up with Bolger and they searched the quarry for Logic – which indicates that he had indeed thought Logic had been killed or injured in the blast.[34]

Logic had not been killed. As the fuse was lit he ran off, not back to the work gang with his companion, but down a creek that led out of the quarry. The confusion of the blast, Bolger's inattention, and Barrien's apparent belief that Logic had been caught up in the explosion, meant that it was some time before they realised that Logic had escaped.

Barrien set off down the creek in pursuit. He caught sight of the prisoner in Theile's wheat paddock. Logic had stripped off most of his clothes and was in the act of throwing his shirt to the ground when Barrien called on him to 'Stand!'. The call was made three times but Logic paid no attention and just ran. Barrien fired three or four times but his bullets missed their mark.

Another prison guard, Brown, was following some distance behind, not yet aware that Barrien had seen Logic. After cresting a hill northeast of the prison Brown met Theile's young daughter, who told him that there was a man in their wheat field. He immediately set off in the direction indicated when he saw, about 400 yards from him, Logic running naked across the field and Barrien firing at him. Brown joined Barrien and together they chased him down a creek in the direction of Modbury, north of Adelaide. The pursuit continued for a few kilometres before they lost him in the trees. With darkness falling, they decided to give up the chase and return to the prison.[35]

Chief Guard Buxton had followed his men to Theile's farm, where the bewildered farmer described the encounter and handed over Logic's prison clothes. Buxton returned to the prison at 7.30 pm and an hour later Barrien and Brown returned with the news that they had failed to recapture the prisoner.[36]

On the night of his escape, after his pursuers had given up their chase, Logic camped under a railway bridge, and the following day made for the ranges near Gawler in the north.[37] For the next few days there were no reports of his whereabouts.

The exact circumstances surrounding Logic's escape were not, at first, made public. According to one report, he had made his break from the work gang while it was being marched back from the quarry.[38] Another account fancifully suggested that Logic had got hold of an old file and worked on his chains so that he could slip them off at the first opportunity.[39] It was several weeks before an accurate account of the escape appeared – in the correspondence columns of the *Adelaide Observer*. The author of the letter used the incident to illustrate the low regard in which Aborigines were held. After describing how Logic was detailed to light the fuse of the dynamite, and how he used the confusion to make his escape, he went on to comment:

> His feelings (although an uncivilized being) may be more easily imagined than described when he learnt the danger he was to run. If he was blown to atoms the warders would not have cared a 'jiff'. Now, I would like to see anyone that would not have acted in a similar way under the circumstances.[40]

Given the guard's reaction when he thought Logic might have been killed or injured, it is a fair appraisal.

Early on the morning of 20 October 1885, hungry and tired after four days on the run, and dressed only in a bed quilt wrapped around his waist, Logic called at a farm near Sheoak Log and asked for a pannikin of flour, which he was given along with some breakfast. He was said to be foot-sore and limping as though wounded. He was no more than 100 kilometres north of Adelaide, mid-way between Gawler and Kapunda. He was unarmed and made no threats against the farmer. Farmer Wear told Logic that he thought he was the escaped prisoner, at which Logic immediately fled. Mounted police immediately descended on the area and began searching the country around Daveytown.[41] Apart from a sighting near Eudunda, Logic disappeared from sight for almost a fortnight.

For much of the time Logic travelled only at night, following what he called the 'wheelbarrow track' north. On a number of occasions he watched the police from a distance, lying low till they were out of sight. It was not until 4 November 1885 that he was seen again, this time in the Never-Never Ranges midway between Georgetown and Jamestown. He was sighted again north of Jamestown, but then he dropped from view for over a week.[42]

On Monday 16 November 1885 Corporal O'Mahony and Mounted Constable Featherstone arrested a man they believed to be Logic near Cotabena station, about fifty kilometres north-east of Hawker. They took him back to Beltana and wired the news to Inspector Besley in Port Augusta. Their prisoner claimed his name was Billabong, and he protested that he had just been released from Port Augusta hospital. A telegram arrived the next morning from Port Augusta confirming that an Aboriginal named Billabong had indeed been discharged from the hospital there. The duo must have felt sure they had captured the notorious Logic as they still refused to allow the convalescing Billabong to go on his way. The entry in their station journal that day reads: 'There being no JP's in township, let "Billabong" out on bail at 10.20 am, charged him with being identical with "Logic". Prisoner one meal.'[43]

The real Logic at this time was still a hundred and fifty kilometres south, having been sighted on 17 November 1885 at a place known as Itali Itali, just south of Quorn.[44] A dozen police and Aboriginal trackers were scouring the area. They were receiving very little help from the locals; indeed, at this stage in Logic's trek public opinion was firmly on his side and farmers were openly helping him. Logic, gaining confidence from that support, was openly approaching people for food. A report in the *Advertiser* on 24 November 1885 detailed Logic's caution and his skill at eluding his pursuers:

> Logic is well on the alert, and when asking for food never gives a chance of surprise from behind. He retraces his steps so cleverly as to defy tracking. He was tracked once for four miles, and five trackers failed to trace him another yard. It will be impossible to capture him in the ranges here, as he could easily distance his pursuers on the rocks.[45]

At the conclusion of the report the correspondent remarked that if Logic evaded capture in the settled districts, it was little wonder he could avoid them in the hills. The writer added, prophetically as it turned out, that Logic 'will probably not be caught until he gets a hundred miles further north'.[46]

From this point of his journey onwards Logic's movements were an open secret to everyone but the police. On the last day of November he visited McNeil's farm, near the town of Wilson. Two days later, on a Wednesday evening, he stopped at John Jarvis's farm near Hawker and was given a meal. On the Thursday he visited two farms, one just south of Hawker and another to the north – perhaps breakfasting at the first and dining at the second. On Friday evening he stayed two hours at Isaac Mill's house, asking only for a drink of water. He was said to be carrying spears and a boomerang, evidently shaped with a tomahawk a settler had given to him, as well as a possum-skin waterbag. He was wearing boots someone else had donated.[47] The settlers were more than kind. One gave him a butcher's knife, another a blanket, and one particularly generous soul gave him a brown tweed suit. 'All gave bread, meat, and tea cheerfully, and tobacco was not grudged either. He is said to have made himself a clay pipe', reported the *Advertiser*.[48]

When in need of food, Logic usually approached the farmhouses at sunset.

According to his own account, the usual formula was, 'Hi, you Logic?' to which he would reply, 'Me Logic.' 'You want him tucker?' would be the next query, and the reply being uniformly in the affirmative he was promptly provisioned and sent on his way with a friendly farewell: 'Good-bye, Logic.'[49]

There were no fear or threats in these meetings, and he was greeted as hospitably by lone women on isolated stations as by men. Logic's treatment is all the more remarkable when you consider that the farmers themselves were suffering a drought that had cursed the colony for a number of years.

While he was being thus entertained by settlers near Hawker, the police, ten in total and four trackers, were lying in wait at the head of Elder's Range near the Arkaba homestead.[50]

Logic left the Hawker area and travelled by night along the coach road to Blinman. He by-passed the police waiting for him in the Elder Range and continued his journey northward. He camped overnight at Wilpena and the next morning, hearing chickens, visited a farmhouse and was fed.[51] That day, 9 December 1885, the *Port Augusta Dispatch* printed a short article that described the generosity of the settlers in the region toward Logic and the sympathy felt for him. It was suggested that, given 'the resolute manner in which he escaped from Yatala, and the determined and persistent style in which he has made his way up to the north', there was good reason to believe he would not be taken without bloodshed. The writer thought that the wisest course was to allow him to escape, and that this was the course the authorities were about to follow: 'a northern correspondent informs us that the pursuit is being relaxed, and will in all probability be altogether abandoned'.[52]

On Wednesday night, 9 December 1885, Logic camped about 20 kilometres short of Blinman, not far from the Parachilna Ochre Mines, famed among Aboriginal people of the north-east for their sacred red ochre. For Logic it may have been familiar country; it is possible that he had made the journey as a young man. The next day as he travelled through the mallee he saw a party of police. As he hid, one group passed him on his left while another passed on the right. Muniah, an Aboriginal tracker employed by the police, did not pass by, so Logic rose and confronted him, boomerang in hand. The *Advertiser* reported what happened next:

When challenged, however, he replied, 'Me no run away,' and submitted quietly, Muniah running up and seizing him by the wrist, and a trooper coming up with the 'bracelets'. When asked why he did not resist he shook his head emphatically, and replied, 'No fight! No fight! See him pistol.'[53]

He later confessed that he thought he would be shot down if he tried to make a run for it, as they had tried to gun him down when he fled from Yatala. After more than 50 days on the run Logic was again in the hands of the police.

On Friday 11 December 1885 hundreds gathered at the Quorn railway station to meet the evening train that they believed would be carrying Logic to Adelaide.[54] On the same evening, and even more optimistically, it was reported that a 'great number' had assembled outside the Adelaide police station to catch a glimpse of the recaptured fugitive.[55] Logic spent the night in police custody at Hawker. On Saturday morning he was taken by train to Quorn, where the disappointed crowds of the previous night were rewarded with his appearance. It seems that despite his police escort he was able to talk to the press and the crowds. He was said to be in good health and very talkative. According to one report he was depressed at the idea of going down to Adelaide and hoped the governor would release him. The correspondent added: 'he will not run short of tobacco, fruit, &c., while at Quorn'.[56] Transportation had changed since his last journey south some five years before. On that occasion he had been taken by horse to Port Augusta and then by boat to Adelaide. This time he travelled by rail. On the Wednesday Logic, in the custody of a constable, left Port Augusta on a goods train bound for Adelaide before being transferred to an ordinary passenger train at Eurelia. It was during this journey that much of Logic's story was revealed: his escape from the stockade, the assistance given him by the northern settlers and the events surrounding his killing of Mulhall and eventual imprisonment. The *Advertiser*'s correspondent reported that he was in good spirits and 'far from being a "bag of bones"', as had been reported, was in 'good training trim'.[57]

On Monday and Tuesday night crowds gathered at the North Terrace railway station to catch a glimpse of Logic but on both occasions they were disappointed.[58] The crowds that assembled at the various stations along the route were said to have represented a cross-section of the community, but especially the working classes. According to the *Adelaide Observer*'s correspondent:

> To be sure the larrikin class were not absent, but they did not compose a very considerable proportion of the crowd, who seemed for the most part to be respectable members of the industrial orders.[59]

On the Wednesday night the sensation of a fire in Grenfell Street drew the crowds away from the station.[60] It was this night that Logic finally arrived back in Adelaide, although he never did appear in the city, being taken from the train at the Dry Creek station and transferred straight to the nearby stockade.[61]

News of Logic's recapture unleashed another flood of letters to the newspapers asking that the governor exercise his prerogative of mercy. There was a sense that Logic had already been treated too harshly for what amounted to no more than a crime of self-defence. Many argued that if they had been in the same situation as Logic they might have done the same. One correspondent wrote of Logic's tormentor, 'I would have shot him down like a dog'.[62] Another criticised the inequity of the legal system itself, portraying Logic as a victim of a system where influence and status counted for more than did justice:

> We might compare the case of Logic with one which occurred here not forty years ago, in which an educated man fired at another who had made no attempt to injure him in any way. He is a big white fellow, and by the influence of one or two escapes with a very short imprisonment. This poor uneducated black gets thrashed and shot at, and, knowing naught of the law, takes it into his own hands to punish his assailant, and after being hunted down drags out a weary life in prison for want of a few influential friends to obtain his release.[63]

One correspondent put it in simple terms: 'Judges and magistrates do not like to be told, that there is one law for the rich and one for the poor'.[64] Another suggested that after his release Logic's 'ingenuity and cleverness' should be rewarded by a government post 'in the taxation or other department'.[65]

Great derision was reserved for the police, whom Logic had made to look foolish in his two months on the run. The Aboriginal trackers were given more credit for Logic's capture than the sergeant who was in charge of the hunt. One person wrote sarcastically that Corporal Mahoney and his men deserved leather medals for their efforts: 'Does this not show the wonderful nerve of our police in venturing an attack on such a wild desperado as Logic?'[66] Another correspondent was more concerned at the damage done to the horses in this 'glorious deed'.[67] Logic had become a hero.

In addition to the letters of support, petitions were hastily organised and presented to the government. On 15 December 1885, while Logic was in custody at Port Augusta, Messrs Fisher, Rymill and Magarey, among other prominent citizens, presented a petition to the chief secretary calling for Logic's release.[68] It had been signed by almost 2000 people. Another petition, signed by about 300 residents of Kapunda, was received by the governor.[69] Logic's fate was even raised in parliament. The Irishman William West-Erskine rose and addressed the assembly on the matter. 'Christmas', he said, 'was approaching, and he felt sure he only expressed the feelings of the community, when he said that he thought mercy might be shown to the unfortunate fellow'. The commissioner of public works rose in response and, unable to avoid the obvious, stated that the case would be taken 'into logical consideration'.[70]

How is it that Logic, a convicted murderer and an Aborigine, became a folk-hero to white South Australians? Logic's luck was to be in the right place at the right time. His popular notoriety was embedded in a felicitous coincidence of social circumstances which saw his case become a convenient symbol of social discontent, at a time when popular and scientific interest in indigenous cultures rendered his Aboriginality a unexpected bonus.

Under the growing influence of evolutionary theory in the 1870s came an international revival of interest in 'primitive' cultures, making Australian Aborigines a fashionable subject of intellectual inquiry.[71] South Australia's response is best exemplified by the work of George Taplin and J.D. Woods. Taplin had been a missionary among the Ngarrindjeri of the Murray River and Lower Lakes district since 1859. By 1870 he was communicating with ethnological societies in England, writing on Aboriginal languages and collecting ethnographic material.[72] His book about the Ngarrindjeri appeared in 1873.[73] Responding to international interest, the government gave Taplin financial support to undertake a comparative study of South Australian Aboriginal culture.[74] The results of this research, based on information gathered from questionnaires distributed throughout the colony, was published in 1879 as *Folklore, Manners, Customs and Languages of the South Australian Aborigines*. In 1879 J.D. Woods edited and introduced a book entitled *The Native Tribes of South Australia* in which he reproduced the more significant ethnographic writings generated in South Australia since settlement. Among the other notable ethnographies of the period was an account of the Diyari of the Lake Eyre region, the district Logic was associated with, and the Bunganditj of the lower south-east.[75] Popular newspapers became interested in the subject and the publications were reviewed and extracts published. The Aborigines, for so long dismissed as the dying race, were suddenly revivified in the colonial imagination as living relics of primeval man.

The scientific reconstruction of the Aborigines overlapped another process: the appropriation of Aboriginality as an icon of emerging colonial nationalism. Evidence of this is apparent in the public response to a series of events in late May and early July 1885, just three months before Logic's escape from Yatala prison. Perhaps perceiving the growing public interest in Aboriginal culture the missionaries of Point MacLeay and Point Pearce missions decided to stage a corroboree in Adelaide as a fund-raiser. Adelaide Oval was hired for Saturday 31 May and a fee of sixpence asked as the price of admission. Much to the surprise of the four policemen on duty that night a crowd estimated at 20,000 attended the event.[76] The performance had to be abandoned when spectators surged onto the oval, almost swamping the dancers. The corroboree took place after police reinforcements were called and order was restored. So successful was the event that a sequel was held at Kensington oval on the following Wednesday before a modest audience of 2000 people. A repeat performance was held on Adelaide oval the following Saturday, in the presence of the governor and a more subdued crowd of 9000 people.[77]

Each event began with the performers, adorned in traditional style, presenting a corroboree and a sham tribal fight, and concluded with their reappearance in western dress and a rendition of the national anthem. The missionaries clearly meant the performances to illustrate the social advancement of their charges, but witnesses to the performance, an urban population with little or no experience of Aboriginal culture, were probably less interested in missionary pedagogy than in the 'exotic primitivism'. Such popular interest in Aboriginal culture had never before been experienced in the colony. Similar performances were held to coincide with South Australia's jubilee celebration in 1886 and Aboriginal exhibits were routinely included in the colony's contribution to the international and intercolonial exhibitions of the period.[78] Aboriginality had become both a commodity and a signifier of provincial identity.

Logic's notoriety must also be understood in the context of bushranging. Ned Kelly had been hanged just five years before Logic's exploits and popular interest in the subject was still high. In January

'Logic – his escape and capture', *The Pictorial Australian*,
January 1886

1886 a full page article in the *Pictorial Australian* told the story of Logic's escape and eventual recapture in great detail, and was accompanied by a portrait of Logic surrounded by cameos of his exploits.[79] Logic's appearance in the illustration is telling; he is portrayed wearing a suit, confidently defying his pursuers and proudly defiant in his eventual recapture. In both the text and illustrations Logic is the underdog receiving aid from sympathetic farmers. Significantly, the article was accompanied by a brief history of bushranging in Australia. Though never described as a bushranger, the 'outlaw' element of his escapades invited such associations. The article, while formally condemning bushrangers as 'vermin', proceeded to glamorise them: 'The fascinations attaching to the wild, roving, albeit rascally life of the free booter often touch a sympathetic cord in the bosom of ancient youth . . .'[80]

This passage is interesting when compared to one of the last comments made in the Logic article:

> [we] shall positively rejoice when we learn, as in a very few days we hope to do, that this hardly-used son of the wilds has been granted the heaven-born boon of freedom, for which, as we all know, he so gallantly strove.[81]

In this account Logic is an individual who has suffered injustice at the hands of the 'authorities' and who deserves his freedom.

The final factor that needs to be taken into account in understanding Logic's celebrity, and perhaps the most important, is that his notoriety occurred in an atmosphere of social discontent. During the 1870s the colony's economy was buoyant; mining and agriculture were booming while public works and urban construction expanded dramatically. This was the period when South Australia's railway network was reaching out to the newly settled agricultural lands in the north. To meet the labour demands assisted immigration was revived and boatloads of Scots, English and Germans were a common sight in the harbour.

The bubble burst with the onset of a recession in 1883–84. A series of drought years in the early 1880s, combined with a drop in prices, badly affected the pastoral industry. Not only was the pastoral industry suffering but the economic conditions led to the closure of mines in the mid-north and a virtual halt to public works. Adding to the already large numbers of unemployed was the stream of migrants who were continuing to arrive, many having arranged their passage up to two years earlier when prospects were brighter.

Social discontent took the form of public meetings to oppose immigration and taxation or to discuss the problems faced by the unemployed, as well as strikes to protest against reductions in wages and public demonstrations on the steps of parliament. The largest demonstration occurred during a bootmakers' strike in the middle of November 1885, a fortnight before Logic was recaptured. Public unrest over the economic crisis reached a peak in the last quarter of 1885, during which time the daily reports of Logic's exploits were nestled between items about public demonstrations and the problems of the unemployed.[82]

The public response to Logic's escape should be judged against this background of economic hardship and anger against the authorities. Many letters to the press appealing for mercy for Logic made direct reference to the economic conditions of the time. One letter, for instance, was headed 'Logic and the Depression' and suggested that the injustice Logic suffered was comparable to that suffered by the many settlers who had been brought out to a colony already facing a surplus of labour.[83] It comes as no surprise that one of the petitions raised on Logic's behalf came from Kapunda, a mining town badly affected by the depression. Logic's case was adopted as a topical and opportune symbol of the suffering being experienced at the hands of heartless authority.

Governor Robinson faced a dilemma. If he pardoned Logic he could be seen to be condoning a gaol-breaker, but if he refused to release him he would be flying in the face of massive public support. A memo from him detailed a compromise:

> If Logic conducts himself well for a month from the time of his re-arrest, I am of opinion that he may be discharged. The offence of breaking prison is so serious a one that it cannot, under any circumstances, be altogether overlooked, and I think that less than the time which I have named would be insufficient to meet the case. At the expiration of that time if the prisoner's conduct remains good he may be pardoned the remainder of his sentence.[84]

A warrant of discharge was issued on 9 December and that day Logic was put on a passenger train to Port Augusta.

On his arrival he was met by Corporal Richards, who took him to the home of Inspector Besley, sub-protector of Aborigines in the north. After a few days with Besley he was put on the Thursday morning train for Beltana, from where he was to walk back to Tinga Tingana. The government gave him a new pair of moleskin trousers, a blue shirt and a water bag, and they returned the swag of goods that he had collected on his last journey north.[85] This was virtually the last the people of Adelaide heard of Logic except for a curious note reprinted from a northern paper on 30 January 1886:

> We understand (says the *Area Express*) a travelling showman, well-known in the North, has made arrangements with Logic, the Roper River black, who has lately received his freedom from the Adelaide Gaol, to take him on a tour through the other colonies. This novel mode of raising the wind will no doubt prove a lucrative employment.[86]

Inspector Besley reported the attempt to take Logic on this tour but unfortunately his letter has long since been destroyed. Nothing more came of the proposal so it seems that the government persuaded Logic, or the showman who had approached him, to drop the idea.[87] Logic was about 30 years of age when he finally returned, a free man, to his own country.

Logic returned briefly to public notice in connection with a murder case that had parallels with his own. In 1889 a stockman named Richard Marrack was killed by his 'blackboy' Jacky near Dulkaninna on the Birdsville track. Jacky was arrested and tried for the crime in Adelaide. Defended by the same man who had represented Logic, Jacky claimed he had killed Marrack in self-defence during a drunken quarrel. While the evidence against him was circumstantial and contradictory, the jury found him guilty of murder, although it recommended mercy. The judge however sentenced him to be hanged.[88]

A public campaign was immediately begun to have the sentence of death commuted: petitions were got up, deputations waited on parliament and letters were sent to the press. Supporters of Jacky pointed out the circumstantial nature of the evidence against him and the harsh treatment he had received after his arrest – being brought to Adelaide in chains. On this occasion the campaigners faced a number of difficulties. It was the festive season and many important players, such as the governor and leading members of the Aborigines Friends Association, were out of town. More significantly, the letters and articles that appeared in the local press in support of Jacky were matched by an equal number insisting upon his guilt and demanding that the sentence be carried out.[89]

The essence of their case was that exemplary justice needed to be shown to prevent any repetition of Marrack's murder and to protect bushmen in isolated districts. One correspondent asked rhetorically: what was the result of the clemency shown Logic on the district in question? He pointed out that after the flooding of the Diamentina in 1887 a white man had been killed on the Clifton Hills run and that the police had done nothing about it. He noted that the previous year an 'old blackfellow' had been murdered on an outstation near Innamincka by a 'mob of blacks headed by Logic', that a few weeks before a settler had been 'compelled to shoot a black in self-defence', and that 'only last week Logic has been assisting to take the life of a blackfellow at Innamincka'. By the correspondent's own account Logic was not the perpetrator of any of these alleged crimes; the most that could be said was that he was guilty by association. The writer's point is that there was a direct causal link between the authority's failure to properly punish Logic and the continuing violence in the district. Imprisonment, he claimed, was the Aborigines' 'dream of bliss': 'Such being the case the Government are offering a reward for murder by not punishing such scoundrels as Jackey and Logic'.[90] Another correspondent suggested that if Jacky was hanged in Adelaide Gaol photographs should be taken of the event and distributed among Jacky's family and friends as a warning.[91]

Similar sentiments were expressed in an article by an *Adelaide Observer* journalist writing under the name 'Hugh Calyptus'. His article purported to present the views of an Aboriginal called Jimmy Warriotta who, we are led to believe, found the white man's justice a source of puzzlement. When it was suggested that he would not have liked to see Logic hang, he is said to have replied:

> 'Baal, no good that one like that. What for white fellow no bin wallop Logic like um overseer do. Him Logic bin tell it tribe no good killum white fellow that way. Plenty whack blackfellow. No me like to see Jacky hung, you plenty thrash um away up North long a blacks. That one plenty make um no killum white fellow. Him bin pull away quick all right, you see.'[92]

This is unlikely to have been the Aboriginal view, but the Aboriginal view was anyway of little consequence to Europeans at the time.

The significance of Jacky's case is that it highlights the singularity of Logic's popular notoriety. Jacky was probably as worthy of public sympathy as Logic, but the other ingredients, that arcane confluence of social and ideological forces, were absent. Perhaps Logic had exhausted them. The irony is that Logic's story, rather than being employed in support of Jacky, was used against him. As it happened, the modest public support for Jacky was sufficient for an eleventh-hour reprieve from the gallows – although he died just two years later from consumption in Yatala Labour Prison.[93]

Logic died in December 1903 and was still sufficiently well remembered to merit an obituary in the *Adelaide Observer*:

DEATH OF A NOTORIOUS BLACKFELLOW

Innamincka, December 26

The once notorious, but now almost forgotten, Logic, the blackfellow, murderer, and gaol breaker, died here last Wednesday. Since returning to these regions after his reprieve, he hardly ever left the district, being always afraid of the whitefellow. He was for some time one of the native police, and was considered a good tracker. He had been ailing for the last twelve months with an internal complaint.[94]

The issue in which the obituary appeared featured a photograph of Logic. His notoriety occurred when he worked as a stockman, and illustrations from that time showed him wearing his prison clothes or the suit that settlers reputedly gave him. The 1904 photograph, however, featured Logic standing naked and brandishing a boomerang – posed as the 'naked savage'.

In 1910 there was a brief reference to Logic in an *Adelaide Observer* article about Harry Bailes, a man described as 'king of the Deerie tribe' and 'a wonderful tracker'. It was Harry Bailes, the correspondent wrote, who 'tracked the notorious Logic to his lair'. While the tone is relatively mild, it conveys a sense of the wild and dangerous days.[95]

Another reference to Logic occurs in the recollections of the bushman Jack Carriage – the reference dates to about 1918. The story according to Carriage was that the head stockman was out with Logic, he had cause to reprimand him during the day and that evening Logic killed him and then disappeared. We are told that Logic returned with a group of Aborigines three years later, was recognised and ran off. When Carriage threatened to turn the whole group in they handed Logic over. The remainder of the story was this:

[Logic] was chained to a cart wheel for the night but managed to get a nail out of the woodwork and picked the lock and escaped. He was again caught and this time was shackled and taken to Beltana where he was tried and given fourteen years gaol. He escaped after five years and was arrested in the Flinders Ranges, while making his way back to his own territory, and returned to gaol. He was later released and as Jack put it 'he had been a good nigger ever since'.[96]

Despite embellishments such as the lock-picking episode, the broad structure of the story is accurate: the murder, eventual capture, escape, recapture and release. What is important is what is left out: notably the circumstances surrounding the stockman's death and the public support Logic received.

An account of Logic's story appeared in a series of reminiscences published in the *Adelaide Observer* in 1928. The author, Allan Ross, worked in the far north during the time that Logic's story unfolded. While he recalled the main events in the story – the murder, recapture, escape and eventual release – the details are rather blurred. The interesting aspect of the article is not that an old squatter's memory had become vague on detail, but that Logic's behaviour conformed with stereotypical images of Aborigines that had been developing as part of Australian folklore from about the 1880s onwards. Of the 'Tragedy at Tinga Tingana', as he called it, he wrote:

At that time a sensation was caused by the murder of Peter Mulholland, head stockman on Tinga Tingana, by his blackboy Logie. It was generally surmised that he was taken unawares and disabled by being stabbed in the temple. Mulholland was a powerful man, and the nigger would have had no show in a fair go.[97]

The article makes no mention of Logic's treatment by Mulhall, nor the public sympathy he received when the full story finally emerged. Logic is simply portrayed as a devious 'nigger' who used treacherous cunning to overpower his victim.

The most substantial reminiscence about Logic appeared in the *Adelaide Chronicle* in August 1937. Published under the heading 'Escape and Death of a Killer', the opening paragraph sets the tone for the rest of the article:

SULLEN NATIVE WHO BEAT JOHN MULHALL TO DEATH

> In this story from real life, 'Far North' tells of the tragic death of
> John Mulhall, an inoffensive man who went outback after having
> trained for the priesthood. The murderer, a sullen, treacherous
> native, Logis, escaped from Yatala, but a few years later met his
> death.[98]

The author describes Logic as a 'brutal killer attended by remarkable
luck' and then goes on to recount his background:

> A native of Queensland, nothing was known of his history until
> the time of the murder. It then transpired that he had been
> employed as a horse boy by several Queensland drovers, but his
> sullen treacherous nature, and frequent desertions soon became
> a bar to his employment. He wandered into South Australia and
> forced himself on the tribes of the Strzlecki Creek . . . Logic soon
> proved himself useless, silent and sullen. He would lag behind the
> white man letting the horses wander where they would while he
> hunted, cooked, and ate lizards and suchlike.

All the while, so the author explains, the patient stockman would
wait at the camp, without provisions or equipment, while Logic made
his lazy way back. Such behaviour caused much inconvenience, 'but no
amount of persuasion could alter the black's dilatory ways' and 'each
cattleman who tried him once would not take him again'. That is, until
Mulhall came along and decided to give him a chance. According to
the author, Mulhall 'should never have been a cattleman': 'soft spoken,
highly educated and trained for the priesthood he was not the stuff
of which cattlemen are made.' The article made much of the contrast
between the 'silent, dour black' and the 'priestly cattleman'; it is as
though the author is defending the image of the bushman by stressing
the inexperience of the new chum.

The article moves on to how the alarm was raised and a search
party organised. Playing up the theme that Logic was an outsider, dis-
liked by both black and white, he writes; 'As Logic was no friend of the
local blacks, there was no difficulty in getting trackers'. The truth, as
indicated by the trial testimony, is that on Logic's return to the station
all the Aborigines except a few fled with him, apparently concerned
about their own safety, let alone Logic's. In this section the author

makes no mention of Logic's beatings at the hands of this 'priestly cattleman' nor of the fact that he had shot Logic in the back. Not only does the author omit this detail, he reverses the truth; in noting that Mulhall's revolver had slipped into the seat of his trousers because he refused to wear a holster, he goes on to observe: 'It was a grim trick of fate that saved Logic from being shot, as his victim possessed a fully loaded revolver'. Logic, of course, had been shot, and Mulhall *did* possess a holster – perhaps it was a show of bravura after shooting Logic that led him to slip his gun casually into the trouser band.

The last section of the article recounts Logic's capture and in the process illustrates the author's contempt of the station Aborigines, whom he portrays as childlike and greedy:

> One morning a group visited the station and told the manager that Logic was in the camp.
>
> 'You bin gibbit plenty flour, plenty tea, plenty sugar, baccy and plenty good old shirt belongs white fellow, we bin catchim that fellow Logic,' they said.
>
> This suggestion was agreed to and sure enough they nabbed Logic while asleep and dragged him struggling to the station followed by half the tribe bristling with spears.

In conclusion the author notes that Logic was sentenced to life imprisonment in Yatala from where he escaped, only to be recaptured and released. The final paragraph presents yet another cliché: 'Bushmen said his death was due to the degrading effects of civilization while living among the white cattlemen'.

The conventional aim of biography is to reveal the character and motives of the subject – that is hardly possible in the case of Logic. Perhaps the closest we get to actually hearing his 'voice' is when Judge Boucaut recorded his interjection during the trial and when the journalist spoke to him on the train back to Adelaide after his re-capture. But what we do have in the record of his public notoriety is an exposition of the way in which the 'other', the marginalised and powerless, is created and maintained in the public consciousness of the dominant culture. In 1878 the initial reports of Mulhall's murder were clothed in fake heroism and distorted by appeals to the convenient stereotype of the 'savage black' on the frontier. In the *Pictorial Australian*'s tabloid version, the story of his escape was given a romantic, bushranging flavour. Logic's notoriety occurred at a time of social discontent, so it was no wonder that an underdog who had been badly treated by the authorities should emerge as a folk-hero. The surprise is that the folk-hero should be Aboriginal. What is less surprising is that with the passage of time, as his story was told as part of the frontier folk-lore of the north, he was reduced again to the simple stereotype of the 'savage black'.

EPILOGUE:
UNSETTLING THE PAST

■

For most of the era of White Australia, from the 1890s to the 1960s, Aboriginal people were subject to discriminatory laws that denied them the rights and privileges of 'ordinary' Australians. Governments wanted Aboriginal people out of sight and out of mind; either segregated on missions and reserves or 'absorbed', through policies of assimilation, into the dominant white culture. Not only was there a presumption that Aboriginal people would die out, but the policies of the era sought to facilitate their disappearance – if not physically, then racially and culturally. In the light of these policies and expectations, it is hardly surprising that national histories should have excluded them.

When the anthropologist W.E.H. Stanner made his challenge to Australians to break the 'great Australian silence' he was writing in the afterglow of the 1967 referendum which, symbolically at least, marked the re-inclusion of Aboriginal people into the conception of the Australian nation. Since that time many scholars have taken up the challenge. The silence has been well and truly broken – to the discomfort of many. The on-going re-evaluation of the national past has revealed many things that generations of white Australians were largely ignorant of: the discriminatory laws that denied Aboriginal people their basic human rights, the policies that saw children being removed from their families, the exploitation of Aboriginal workers in the pastoral industry and, perhaps most important of all, the myth of *terra nullius*.

This reassessment of the past has had a profound effect not only on the politics of the nation, but on the way we see ourselves as a nation – the two, of course, being inexorably linked. The new history of what Bain Attwood has referred to as the 'Aboriginal colonial past' has had

an 'unsettling' effect, challenging the foundational narratives that generations of Australians have taken for granted.[1] As Attwood has argued,
these narratives prescribed particular roles and relationships for the
'British', the 'Australians' and the 'Aborigines'. If the British heritage
provided a source of legitimacy, their descendants – the Australians –
built upon that foundation and forged a modern, progressive nation,
while the 'Aborigines' were cast as primitive and unchanging relics
of an earlier age of man. The 'new Australian history', Attwood con-
tends, 'reveals the conservatives' assumption that the mere return of the
Aboriginal past necessarily entails the displacement of the British one,
and so betrays the extent to which their traditional history depended
and depends upon the silencing of Aboriginal narratives'.[2]

Given the way particular narratives of the past serve to legitimate
contemporary political actions, it is hardly surprising that critics of
native title, or opponents of an apology for the stolen generations, have
defended the traditional narratives. Purveyors of the 'new history' have
been stigmatised as promoting a 'black arm-band' view of the past, or
surrendering to 'political correctness'. Defenders of the 'old history'
have, among other things, bluntly denied the violence of the frontier,
justified the removal of Aboriginal children on the grounds that it was
done with the best of intentions or, more crudely, by raising issues such
as cannibalism, endeavoured to reinstall a view of Aboriginal savagery
and implicitly to re-enthrone the notion of settlement as a necessary
and benevolent introduction of civilisation.

Where the defenders of the 'old history' have been unable to defend
the actions of our forebears, they have slipped into a sort of historical
schizophrenia, insisting, one moment, that we forget the past, and
the next that we celebrate it. Former Deputy Prime Minister Fischer,
for instance, acknowledged that there had been 'horrific massacres'
in the past, but called upon us to put these things behind us on the
grounds that 'the horrors of the past were not caused by this generation of Australians'.[3] Those who would call upon us to forget the past
demand, in other contexts, that we remember it: that we celebrate the
sacrifice of our soldiers, the heroism of our pioneers, and the deeds of
the nation's great men and women. Should we, in the interests of fair-
ness, forget these things? What, in the interests of justice, should we
remember? These are ultimately false dichotomies: the horrors are just
as much a part of our past as the deeds of glory. Our challenge is to
reconcile them.

NOTES

■

INTRODUCTION: THE VIOLENCE OF MEMORY

1   Rodney Cockburn, *Pastoral Pioneers of South Australia*, Vol. I (Lynton Publications, Adelaide, 1974, facsimile of the original by Publishers Limited, Adelaide, 1925–27), p. 140–141.

2   *House of Commons, Sessional Papers*, 1836, 39, no. 426. First Annual Report of the Colonization Commissioners of South Australia, p. 8.

3   B. Dickey & P. Howell, *South Australia's Foundation: Select Documents* (Wakefield Press, Adelaide, 1986), p. 43.

4   R.H.W. Reece, *Aborigines and Colonists: Aborigines and Colonial Society in New South Wales in the 1830s and 1840s*, (Sydney University Press, Sydney, 1974), p. 130.

5   *House of Commons. Sessional Papers*, 1837, 7, no. 425, Report of the Select Committee on Aborigines (British Settlements), p. 77.

6   *South Australian Register*, 3 June 1837.

7   For instance, the comments of the settler John Brown, Diary, 13 February 1837, p. 75, Mortlock Library Nos. 36–37; *South Australian Register*, 27 April 1839; *Southern Australian*, 7 April 1843.

8   A. Grenfell Price, *The Foundation and Settlement of South Australia*, (Preece, Adelaide, 1924) p. 95.

9   A. Pope, *Resistance and Retaliation: Aboriginal-European Relations in Early Colonial South Australia*, (Heritage Action, Bridgewater, SA, 1989), pp. 57–59, 66–71, 86–91, 93–97.

10   *Southern Australian*, 8 May 1839.

11   Ibid.

12   Ibid.

13   J.C. Hawker, *Early Experiences in South Australia*, (E.S. Wigg & Son, Adelaide, 1899), p. 12.

14   E. Eyre, *Journal of Expeditions of Discovery into Central Australia and Overland from Adelaide to King George's Sound*, (T & W Boone, London, 1845), p. 170.

15   *Adelaide Observer*, 5 August 1843.

16   John Wrathall Bull, *Early Experiences of Colonial Life in South Australia* (E.S. Wigg & Son, Adelaide, 1878), p. 69.

17   J.F. Hayward, 'Reminiscences of Johnson Frederick Hayward', *Proceedings of the Royal Geographical Society of Australasia, SA Branch*, Vol. 29, 1929, p. 147.

18   E. Mahony, Reminiscences published in the *Proceedings of the Royal Geographical Society of Australia, SA Branch*, Vol. 28, p. 70–71.

19   H. Reynolds, *The Other Side of the Frontier*, (University of Queensland Press, St Lucia, Qld, 1981), is the best known modern reassessment of frontier violence.

20   See, for instance, *South Australian Register*, 10 November 1838; 2 November 1839; 22 February 1840; 18 September 1847; 6 March 1852.

21 *Adelaide Observer*, 12 December 1863.
22 C. Sturt, 'An account of the sea coast and interior of South Australia', in *Journal of the Central Australian Expedition, 1844–45* (London, 1849) p. 190.
23 Hayward, p. 88.
24 J. Watts, *Family Life in South Australia* (W.K. Thomas & Co., Adelaide, 1890), p. 175.
25 GRG 24/6/1906/1846.
26 Tom Griffiths, 'Past Silences: Aborigines and Convicts in our History Making', in Penny Russell and Richard White (eds), *Pastiche 1: Reflections on nineteenth century Australia* (Allen & Unwin, Sydney, 1994), p. 11.
27 Reynolds, p. 121.
28 Ibid.
29 Ibid., p. 122.
30 The estimate is based upon a preliminary survey of European deaths reported in newspapers and court records.
31 W.E.H. Stanner, *After The Dreaming* (Australian Broadcasting Corporation, Sydney, 1991), p. 24.
32 W. Murdoch, *The Making of Australia: An Introductory History* (Whitcombe & Tombs, Melbourne, 1929?), pp. 9–10.
33 Chris Healy, *In the Ruins of Colonialism* (Cambridge University Press, Cambridge, 1997), p. 123.
34 Cockburn, Forward.
35 J.B. Hirst, 'The Pioneer Legend', in John Carroll (ed.), *Intruders in the Bush* (Oxford University Press, Melbourne, 1986), p. 15.
36 Ibid., pp. 14–15.
37 Cockburn, p. 133.

RECONSTRUCTING THE MARIA MASSACRE

1 'Milmenrura' (Melmenrura, Milmenroora), 'the Big Murray tribe'and the 'McGrath Flat tribe' are names attributed to the people of the Coorong region in the colonial records.
2 The Advocate General, Minute to the Council, 15 September 1840, published in the *Register*, 19 September 1840, p. 4.
3 Ibid.
4 Governor Gawler, Minute to the Council, 15 September 1840, published in the *Register*, 19 September 1840, p. 4.
5 Gawler's instructions to the Commissioner of Police, 14 August 1840. O'Halloran papers GRG 5/83. State Records, Adelaide. The orders were also published in the *South Australian Register*, 19 September 1840, p. 4.
6 Ibid.
7 Diary of Thomas O'Halloran 1840–41, O'Halloran papers, GRG 83/5. State Records, Adelaide.
8 Minute to Council, 30 September 1840, published in the *Register*, 3 October 1840, p. 4.
9 Ibid.
10 'A Colonus', letter to the *Register*, 26 September 1840, p. 2.
11 *Register*, 12 September 1840.
12 *Register*, 3 October 1840, p. 4.
13 Ibid.
14 'A Briton', letter to the *Register*, 26 September 1840, p. 2.
15 Mary Thomas, *The Diary and Letters of Mary Thomas 1836–1866*, ed. Kevan Kyffin Thomas (W.K. Thomas & Co., Adelaide, 1925), p. 169.
16 Extract published in the *Adelaide Chronicle*, 30 June 1841.
17 'A Colonist of 1836', the *Register* 26 September 1840, p. 2.

18 Tindale recounting the Ngarrindjeri explanation offered by Milerum, a Ngarrindjeri elder (*Advertiser*, 7 April 1934, p. 11). Tindale's recording of Ngarrindjeri oral history is also noted in *Survival in Our Own Land*, which describes the government action as one of 'the most shameful episodes in the history of the British settlement of "South Australia"', and concludes: 'The Milmenrura had already experienced violent treatment from whalers, sealers and overlanders who abducted their women. When *Maria* sailors began interfering with their women, the Milmenrura men reacted accordingly, attacking to protect their families'. Christobel Mattingly and Ken Hampton, Eds. *Survival in Our Own Land: 'Aboriginal' Experiences in 'South Australia' since 1836* (Wakefield Press, Netley, 1988), p. 37.

19 Lola Cameron-Bonney, response to the article 'Black Wars on the Coorong' in the *Australasian Post*, 13 February 1988. *The Anthropological Society of South Australia*, Vol. 25, no. 8 (1988), pp. 3–4.

20 John Wrathall Bull, *Early Experiences of Colonial Life in South Australia* (Adelaide, 1878), p. 31.

21 'Recollections of a Septuagenarian', *Register* 20 February 1878, p. 18.

22 J.W. Bull, pp. 130–131, 144.

23 John Bowyer Bull, *Reminiscences*. PRG 507 Mortlock Library, Adelaide.

24 J.W. Bull, p. 131.

25 Alexander Tolmer, *Reminiscences of an Adventurous and Chequered Career at Home and at the Antipodes*, in 2 vols. (Sampson Low, Marston, Searle & Rivington, London, 1882), Vol. 1, p. 193.

26 Hailes, p. 18 and J.W. Bull, p. 131.

27 Robert Dixon, *Writing the Colonial Adventure* (Cambridge University Press, Cambridge, 1995), p. 1.

28 Hailes, p. 17.

29 J.W. Bull, p. 146.

30 Tolmer, p. 187. The decidedly military (rather than civil) zeal with which Tolmer engaged in punitive expeditions is expressed by the irritation he recalls in injuring his thumb during the first days of the march to the Coorong, an event which then 'disable[d] me from using my sword' (p. 182). His military approach to relations with Aboriginal people emerges again some chapters later, when recounting his response to the plan of a police expedition to the Rufus River against the Maraura people in August 1841: 'I said if I thought the natives would fight, nothing would give me greater pleasure than to have the satisfaction of punishing the villains for the outrages and murders they had committed; but as there was no probablity of such an event [the new Governor Grey having forbidden the use of firearms], I begged someone else might be sent in my stead' (p. 233).

31 The reader's cue to recognise the narrative as 'reminiscence' is established by appeal to the memory of 'an old settler'. 'A Native Massacre' by 'A South Australian', from the *Adelaide Observer*, republished by the *Register*, 7 September 1868, pp. 3–4.

32 Ibid.

33 Henry Dudley Melville, 'Reminiscences' in 5 Volumes. D6976 Mortlock Library, Adelaide. The handwritten narrative is undated but was probably produced in 1889, since Melville states that he was born in 1827 and was aged 62 at the time of writing.

34 Kay Schaffer, *In the Wake of First Contact: The Eliza Fraser Stories* (Cambridge UP, Cambridge, 1995), p. 107.

35 Melville, p. 14.

36 The story of Eliza Fraser's shipwreck off the Queensland coast in 1836 and her subsequent 'captivity' by and escape from 'savages' circulated, as Kay Schaffer argues, throughout the colonial world (Schaffer, p. 1). The more speculative story of a White Woman of Gippsland entered into popular circulation, as Robert Dixon has argued, from the mid-1840s (Dixon, p. 47). Both stories are, then, more or less contemporaneous with the *Maria* episode.

37 See for example Robert Dixon (1995), Kay Schaffer (1995) and Kate-Darian-Smith, ed. *Captive Lives: Australian Captivity Narratives* (Sir Robert Menzies Centre for Australian Studies, London, 1995).

38 In contrast, of course, the sexual use of black women by white men was taken to be (at least amongst men) an accepted aspect of life beyond the settled districts.

39 Melville's use of the term 'chief', like other Australian colonial references to Aboriginal 'chiefs', places local captivity and other contact stories in parallel with earlier North American colonial narratives.

40 Melville, p. 21.

41 *Advertiser*, 7 April 1934, p. 11.

42 Eliza Davies, *The story of an Earnest Life: a Woman's Adventures in Australia and in Two Voyages around the World* (Central Book Concern, Cinncinati, 1881). Her version of the story was republished recently as 'Eliza Arbuckle's Narrative' in Charles Sturt, *The Mount Bryant Expedition 1839* (Sullivan's Cove, Adelaide, 1982) and page references are to this later text.

43 The truth of this particular story is made questionable not only by the function of Davies' book as popular entertainment, but also by the fact that her companion in this episode – Julia Gawler – does not mention any such event in her own record of the expedition (also published in Charles Sturt, *The Mount Bryant Expedition 1839*).

44 Davies, pp. 58–59.

45 Ibid., p. 51.

46 Ibid., p. 55.

47 Ibid., p. 55.

48 Christina (Mrs James) Smith, *The Booandik Tribe of South Australian Aborigines* (E. Spiller, Adelaide, 1880).

49 Ibid., Preface; p. 33.

50 Smith relates Aboriginal responses to the *Maria* episode of 1840 (p. 24) and the Guichen Bay/ Avenue Range massacre of 1849 (p. 62), as well as to many other instances of casual settler violence.

51 Smith, p. 25.

52 Simpson Newland, *Paving the Way: A Romance of the Australian Bush* (Gay & Bird, London, 1893).

53 Rick Hosking, 'Can the Antipodes Meet? Simpson Newland's *Paving the Way* and Late Nineteenth Century Ideas about the (South) Australian Nation' (unpublished seminar paper, Flinders University 1996), pp. 19–23.

54 Newland, pp. 18–19.

55 Newland, pp. 20–21.

56 Hosking, p. 19.

57 Newland, pp. 16–17.

58 Newland, p. 91.

59 The massacre is presumed to have been perpetuated by the station's owner James Brown. The massacre and its representations are discussed at length in 'The Legend of James Brown'.

60 Newland, p. 70.

61 Newland, 'Aborigines I Have Known', *Proceedings of the Royal Geographical Society, South Australia Branch*.

62 Simpson Newland, *Memoirs of Simpson Newland, C.M.G. Sometime Treasurer of South Australia* (F.W. Preece and Sons, Adelaide, 1926), p. 160.

63 Paul Carter, *The Road to Botany Bay: An Exploration of Landscape and History* (Alfred A. Knopf, New York, 1988), p. xvi.

REGIONAL HISTORY AND THE RUFUS RIVER CONFLICTS

1   *Australian*, 11 May 1994, cited by Rick Hosking, unpublished seminar paper, Flinders University 1996.

2   Maraura is the name given in earlier records to the people of the Lake Victoria/Upper Murray region, the country of the Barkindji people, near its south-western border with Meru country (Australian Institute of Aboriginal and Torres Strait Islander Studies, *Encyclopaedia of Aboriginal Australia*).

3   R. Reece has speculated that the Maraura, who would clash with overland groups throughout 1841, were exerting guerilla warfare on invading Europeans. R. Reece, *Aborigines and Colonists: Aborigines and Colonial Society in New South Wales in the 1830s and 1840s* (University of Sydney Press, Sydney, 1974), p. 25.

4   Deposition of Henry Inman, *Papers Relative to South Australia* (PRSA) No. 87/Encl. 1.

5   Entry 27 April 1841. Diary of Thomas O'Halloran, GRG 5/81. State Records, Adelaide.

6   Entry 30 April 1841. Ibid.

7   Entry 13 May 1841. Diary of James Hawker, PRG 201/1. Mortlock Library, Adelaide.

8   Henry Field to George Hall, Governor's Secretary, 20 May 1841. PRSA No. 87/Encl. 4.

9   John Morphett, et al, to Grey, 24 May 1841. PRSA No. 87/ Encl. 5. This petition and Alfred Langhorne's letter of appeal were published alongside Grey's response in the *Register*, 29 May 1841.

10   Despatch from Grey to Lord Russell, 3 August 1841. PRSA No. 94.

11   Robert Gouger for Grey, response to Memorialists. PRSA No. 87/Encl. 6. Published in the *Register*, 29 May 1841.

12   *Register* 29 May 1841. Although it was not unusual for the *Register* to comment in favour of indigenous rights, the editor George Stevenson's clear swipe at Gawler may have as much to do with the fact that Gawler had transferred the government's printing commission to the *Southern Australian*, as it had to do with his actions in the Milmenrura affair.

13   'The Natives – Suggestions of Captain Grey' in the *Register* 18 April 1840. Those, like Grey, who saw a path to humanitarian policy in the principle of Aboriginal subjecthood did not question that principle's desirability to Aboriginal people. Matthew Moorhouse came closest to doing so when, as part of his quarterly report three months earlier, he wrote: '[there] appears to be moral injustice in imposing the British constitution upon Aboriginal tribes, except in so far as the law of these tribes agree with it'; indeed, such an imposition 'may be viewed as a plea for oppression, for there can be no justice in receiving European evidence against a native, and rejecting, under every circumstance, native evidence against a European'. Report of the Protector of Aborigines, 20 February 1841. PRSA, No. 97.

14   Memorandem to O'Halloran and Moorhouse, 31 May 1841. GRG 5/83. State Records, Adelaide.

15   Moorhouse's report of Charles Langhorne's verbal account to the police party states that five Aboriginal men were shot dead by the overlanders (Moorhouse's report to Grey, 30 June 1841, PRSA No. 92/Encl. 2); news of these deaths does not appear in Langhorne's official report to Major O'Halloran (22 June 1841, PRSA No. 92/Encl. 3) or in O'Halloran's report to Grey (27 June 1841, GRG 5/82. State Records, Adelaide).

16   Entries 22–23 June, Diary of Thomas O'Halloran, GRG 5/81. State Records, Adelaide.

17   Alfred Langhorne had refused to supply meat to the party from the cattle they had recovered. James Hawker, letter to the *Register*, 24 July 1841.

18   John Ellis to Grey, 23 July 1841. PRSA No. 94/Encl.2.

19   Grey's Minute to the Council of Government, 10 July 1841. PRSA No. 94/Encl. 1.

20   Memorandum from Grey to Moorhouse, 3 August 1841. PRSA No. 94/Encl. 7.

21   First report from Moorhouse to Grey, 4 September 1841. PRSA No. 97, Encl. 1.

22   James Hawker, *Early Experiences in South Australia* (E.S. Wigg & Son, 1899), p. 79

23 Proceedings of the Meeting of the Bench of Magistrates, 20–22 September 1841. PRSA No.98/ Enclosure.

24 The second edition of J.W. Bull's *Early Experiences* (1884) left out the personal-centred authorial preface and included an appended 'Extended Colonial History', suggesting that after its first edition the book was marketed not so much as a memoir but rather as a history of South Australia. It has been received as such well into the twentieth century; for instance, the information on the Rufus river clashes provided by the Research Notes series of the State Library of South Australia uses Bull's text as its primary historical resource ('Notes on Attacks on Overlanders by Natives from the Upper Murray', Mortlock Library Research Notes No. 36, undated).

25 J.W. Bull, p. 31.

26 Paul Carter, *The Road to Botany Bay: An Exploration of Landscape and History* (Alfred A. Knopf, New York, 1988), p. xvi.

27 Ibid.

28 In South Australia the Centenary publications of 1936 are repeatedly marked by this metaphor, particularly in relation to the dominance of the colonist and the 'disappearance' of Aboriginal peoples. *The Royal Geographical Society Proceedings* Centenary Supplement, for instance, comments: 'Into the story, in a vague and shadowy way, came those pleasant, pathetic, nomadic people, the aborigines. As we occupied the stage they receded from it' (Vol 34, p. 14). An article in the *Advertiser*'s Special Centenary Issue (September 1, 1936) evokes the same image in reference to the colonist/Aboriginal relationship: 'These, then, were the people who flitted, like dusky shadows, across the background of a stage on which was enacted the drama of the settlement of the colony'.

29 John Bowyer Bull, *Diary of an overland journey north of Streaky Bay for pastoral land* (May–June 1864), with interpretative notes by John Wrathall Bull. PRG 507/1. Mortlock Library, Adelaide.

30 These included Henry Inman's account of the initial conflict, Grey's instructions for the third expedition, Matthew Moorhouse's report on the massacre and the Inquiry's proceedings.

31 In his memorandum to Major O'Halloran before the third expedition to the Murray, for instance, Grey instructed the Police Commissioner to ascertain from the 'hostile tribe' whether their acts of aggression were 'acts of rapine only, or whether they have been committed in order to revenge wrongs previously inflicted upon the natives by other overland parties'. Certainly Matthew Moorhouse expected to find the latter; in his second and longer report to Grey after the August massacre, he condemned the overlanders' sexual use of Aboriginal women and their failure to fulfil promises of reciprocity, and concluded: 'These breaches of moral rectitude on the part of the Europeans have, I fear, been the source of so many disasters to the overland parties'. Even O'Halloran, despite his belief that military action was the most appropriate response to Aboriginal aggression, was in a position to acknowledge the cause behind Aboriginal attacks on overlanders; his journal account of the first expedition in April notes that 'From what I can gather from some of the men who came overland – several Natives have been killed upon different occasions'. Interestingly, although various reasons were enlisted to explain Aboriginal rancour towards overlanders – desire for stock, revenge for previous acts of violence or the sexual exploitation of women – no one imagined that those reasons might include resistance to territorial invasion.

32 J.W. Bull, pp. 54, 67, 71, 179.

33 Susan Sheridan, *Along the Faultlines: Sex, Race and Nation in Australian Women's Writing 1880s–1930s* (Allen and Unwin, St Leonards, 1995), p. 123.

34 Recounting the initial conflict between the Aboriginal and Inman's parties in his diary, Hawker tells the (privately circulated?) story of a shepherd who 'plays dead' in order to escape further attack, and who travels through hostile territory for a week with several spear wounds and with nothing to eat other than a dog's carcase. Bull attributes this story to Inman's published report, with some elaborated detail (pp. 147–48).

35   J.W. Bull, p. 156.
36   See Robert Dixon, *Writing the Colonial Adventure: Race, Gender and Nation in Anglo-Australian Popular Fiction 1875–1914* (Cambridge University Press, Cambridge, 1995).
37   J.W. Bull, p. 163.
38   Compare the 24 June entries of Hawker (PRG 209/1, Mortlock Library) and O'Halloran (GRG 5/81, State Records), with J.W. Bull, p. 165.
39   J.W. Bull, p. 165.
40   The story of the dog's faithfulness, cited by Bull, appears in both Hawker's and O'Halloran's diaries, as well as in O'Halloran's official report (PRSA No. 92/ Encl. 1).
41   J.W. Bull, p. 165.
42   Ibid.
43   Moorhouse paraphrases Langhorne's verbal report of the conflict: 'The natives soon began to throw spears, and we commenced firing amongst them. The fight lasted about 20 minutes; and the result was, death of four of our party and five blacks'. Moorhouse's report to Grey, 30 June 1841. GRG 24/90/393. State Records, Adelaide. In its issue of 17 July 1841, the *Register*'s editor George Stevenson wrote: 'We have been obligingly favoured with the Report by Mr Moorhouse, Protector of the Aborigines, of his expedition to the Murray River natives. Major O'Halloran's report, however, already before the public, comprises the whole affair; and the Protector's report is consequently not possessed of sufficient interest to authorise us to repeat an indifferent version of the same story'.
44   Editor George Stevenson called to colonists not 'to be led away by any harsh and unnecessary feelings of hostility to the Natives'. *Register*, 6 July 1841.
45   'I conceive it becoming all old colonists . . . to give their decided opinion that the punishment inflicted was fully justified by the peculiar circumstances surrounding the case, and with the object of preventing a repetition of such horrors, and which object has been successfully attained' (J.W. Bull, p. 131).
46   J.W. Bull, p. 157.
47   Ibid., p. 163.
48   Ibid., pp. 64–65.
49   Ibid., p. 157.
50   Ibid., p. 171.
51   Proceedings of the Inquiry, 20–22 September 1841. PRSA No. 98/ Enclosure.
52   J.W. Bull, p. 176.
53   Lord Stanley to Governor Grey, 13 May 1841. PRSA No. 100.
54   Compare Bull, p. 146, to Tolmer, p. 217.
55   See for instance Henry Reynolds' recent book *This Whispering in our Hearts* (Allen and Unwin, St Leonards, 1998).
56   J.W. Bull, p. 64.
57   Ibid.
58   J.W. Bull, p. 65. On this point Bull's narrative varies. While he reaffirms the 'infrequency' of crimes against South Australian Aboriginal peoples 'compared with other communities in this part of the world' (p. 73), he also writes that crimes against Europeans 'were exceeded far in atrocity by others committed on the natives' (2nd. Ed., p. 71).
59   Ibid., pp. 65, 176.
60   John Bowyer Bull, *Reminiscences*. PRG 507 Mortlock Library, Adelaide.
61   Ibid.
62   Bull, pp. 178–181. Although Bull's scheme for Aboriginal land title, based on the Poonindie mission township which was established in 1850, may rank him as a liberal thinker for his day, it is, inevitably, underwritten by an assimilationist agenda which does not challenge the invaders' rights to the land. Indeed, even as he provisionally declares the country as Aboriginal-owned

(p. 178), Bull assumes its availability to the colonial administration either for distribution to settlers or for return to its traditional occupants.

63 Ibid., p. 68.
64 Ibid., p. 31.

RECALLING THE ELLISTON INCIDENT

1   Betty Mac, 'The Massacre That Mangultie Did Not Forget', *Mail*, 30 April 1932, p. 16e. I am grateful to Mr Geoffrey Manning for information about this version of the story. His Geoffrey H. Manning, *Manning's Places Names of South Australia* (G.H. Manning, Adelaide, 1990) is an invaluable reference.

2   In the Betty Mac version of the story Mangultie survives and then later takes his revenge by murdering a shepherd near Mount Joy (now Mount Parapet?), his victim a tailor who was attacked while making a wedding garment. This is a fascinating accretion to the traditional details of the 'legend'. She seems to refer to 1930s memories of the murder of William Walker, whom D.R. Myers insists was murdered while making his uncle a wedding suit. In his 'Reminiscences of a Pioneer, born 1846', the typescript held in the Baillie papers in the Mortlock Library (PRG 458/7/7) Myers notes that 'near Lake Hamilton, stands, beside the main road, a lone chimney. At this hut many years ago, a woman was murdered by the natives, and still further west, at Mount Joy, William Walker, too, fell a victim to a native spear (14).' Possibly the woman he has in mind is Anne Easton, who features in other versions of the Elliston incident. A 'John' Walker is buried in the Lake Hamilton cemetery with Ann Easton. See Maureen and Bill Nosworthy *Tjeiringa: The Story of the Sheringa District* (The Sheringa History Committee, Adelaide, 1988), p. 30. I can find no reference to the murder of a William Walker in the *Guide to Records Relating to Aboriginal People*, 5 vols, (State Records, Adelaide, 1988). The former west coast policeman Samuel Dixon records the same story in 1926. Samuel Dixon, 'The Waterloo Bay Massacre', *Register*, 29 March 1926, p. 13f. In 1861 a Mrs Impett was murdered at Mount Joy by two Aboriginal men, Karabidne and Mangeltie, who were both convicted and hanged at Chiriroo on 14 September 1861. *Register*, 19 September 1861, p. 2g. See Robert Hull, 'Waterloo Bay', *Register*, 9 April 1926, p. 13d who also mentions the murder of Mrs Impett. Thus in the absence of communal agreement and knowledge about the past does a story continue to accrete.

3   Neil Thompson, *The Elliston Incident* (Robert Hale, London, 1969). Thompson was born in Ceduna, is descended from an old Streaky Bay family and is the co-author with his wife, Val, of the Centenary History of the Streaky Bay District Council. The dust cover of the novel featured in an Adelaide *News* article about the controversy over the 'incident'. See Jeff Turner, 'What Did Happen at Waterloo Bay?', 2 April 1970, pp. 12–13.

4   'H-,' 'Mystery "Massacre" of Aborigines', *Chronicle*, 18 July 1935, p. 14.

5   John Hamp and his family (including his one-year-old son John Chipp Hamp) arrived in South Australia in 1838 in the *Duke of Roxburgh*. Father and son went to the Port Lincoln district in 1844 (*Observer*, 9 December 1905, p. 28). Hamp's Hill, near Elliston, is named after the father, as is the lake south of Waterloo Bay where one version of the Elliston massacre is said to have begun, where the party of Europeans disturbed a party of Aborigines (*Across the Bar to Waterloo Bay: Elliston 1878–1978*, 1978, p. 10). For clarity's sake, the father is named John Hamp, the son John Chipp Hamp, although it seems they both shared the same name.

6   William Pinkerton was licensed by Charles Driver to 'occupy grazing land at Franklin Harbour on 29 September 1846, at Wedge Hill on 20 May 1847 and at Lake Newland on 30 September 1847'. Jack Casanova, *Fading Footprints: Pioneers, Runs & Settlement of the Lower Eyre Peninsula* (The Author, Port Lincoln, 1992) p. 30. No doubt he did not take up all three leases. Casanova suggests that he was active in establishing a run at Lake Newland 'by 1845 or early 1846. . . .

Pinkerton's station centred on Talia and his wool was shipped each year from the beach inside
Venus Bay' (Casanova, 1992, p. 30).

7   Charles Driver's account of the affray appears in a letter dated 23 August 1848, GRG 24/90/424.
    See also GRG 24/6/1848/1415. State Records, Adelaide.

8   James Geharty's Police Report (dated 28 August 1848) can be found in GRG 24/6/1848/1415.
    State Records, Adelaide. George Stewart seems to have been involved in more than one 'collision'
    with Aboriginal people and if there was indeed a covert massacre in 1849 he might well have
    been implicated. James Geharty was born in Ireland in 1816 and arrived in South Australia on
    the *Pestonjee Bomanjee* in 1838. He arrived in the Port Lincoln district in 1839 as an assistant to B.
    Pratt Winter, the first surveyor to work on Eyre Peninsula (Casanova, 1992, p. 18). He became a
    policeman and after serving at Port Lincoln, he later moved to the Cherriroo Police Station near
    Venus Bay. In 1856 he accompanied Thomas Horne and Alfred King on an exploration trip of
    the Streaky Bay district for Price Maurice. About 1856 he retired from the force and took up
    a pastoral lease on 9 October 1856 for ten square miles on the shores of Venus Bay (lease 625).
    Later he had a lease at Lake Newland (lease no. 507). He died at Marryatville on 30 December
    1897. Mount Geharty north of Cowell is named after him (Manning, 1990, p. 124, 320). The
    spelling of Geharty's name has given many writers real problems over the years.

9   It is very difficult now to be consistent with the spelling of the names of the various individuals
    cited as perpetrators or witnesses in these several cases. Written reports from Charles Driver, the
    Government Resident, Matthew Moorhouse, the Protector of Aborigines, Corporal Geharty,
    Police Superintendent George Dashwood, Nathaniel Hailes, Inspector Tolmer and Sub-Protector
    Clamor Schürmann (to name just some of the commentators) often use different phonetic spell-
    ings when naming the various participants.

10 Charles Driver was originally a pastoralist at Nairne in the 1830s, then moved to the Port Lincoln
    district c. 1839. He gave up his station in March 1842 when he was appointed Government
    Resident and Stipendiary Magistrate. Nathaniel Hailes was his clerk. Driver died on 7 January
    1854. Rodney Cockburn, *Pastoral Pioneers of South Australia* (Publishers Limited, Adelaide,
    1925/7), Vol. 2, p. 249. Driver was the target of a very pointed letter from the Colonial Secretary
    dated 19 April 1884, in which he was reprimanded for his reports upon the subject of the
    natives which had 'neither been copious nor frequent'. He was reminded that 'one of the most
    important duties of the Resident . . . is to exercise a constant and active supervision over the
    welfare and conduct of the natives . . . [I]f the settlers do not find in the activity and energy of
    the Government Authorities sufficient protection from outrages on the part of the Aborigines,
    they will undoubtedly, from a desire of self-defence, take the law into their own hands' (GRG
    24/6/1844/634, State Records, Adelaide). After 1844 his reports are much more detailed – in fact
    there is no other subject described in such detail and at such length as his letters on 'the welfare
    and conduct of the natives'.

11 A book about South Australian colonial experience published in London in 1846 records a
    detailed account of an arsenic poisoning on a 'sheep station at Port Lincoln', the alleged perpe-
    trator the subject of an investigation by the government resident. It seems Dwyer was not the
    first to attempt to murder Indigenous people through labelling poisoned flour. See E. Lloyd,
    A Visit to the Antipodes with some reminiscences of a sojourn in Australia, by A Squatter (Smith Elder &
    Co., London, 1846), pp. 124–126.

12 Captain James Rigby Beevor was a veteran of the Peninsula War, serving in a regiment of Lancers
    under Sir de Lacy Evans and General Bacon. He arrived in South Australia with his brothers
    (one of whom was a pensioner of the East India Company) in the late 1830s. Beevor took up
    land around Mount Barker (Mount Beevor is named after him) where he was involved in an
    incident in which one of his men shot an Aboriginal man (Cockburn, 1927, Vol. II, p. 180–81).
    He also had property on the Hindmarsh River (Cockburn 1927, Vol. II, 180–81; Cockburn,
    1984, p. 22). Dr Neil Draper suggests that there is some anecdotal evidence that Beevor was also
    involved in 'collisions' on Hindmarsh Island (Pers. Comm. 1996). In 1841 Beevor, because of his

military background, was placed in charge of a party of 37 volunteers who joined with a further 27 policemen under Major O'Halloran in a punitive expedition against Aborigines in the 'disturbed districts' around Lake Bonney, where overlanding stock parties had been 'grievously attacked by hordes of niggers', as Cockburn tastefully puts it (Cockburn, 1926, Vol II, p. 181). They rescued the overlanding survivors of the stock parties and their cattle, and a number of Aborigines were killed.

13   Alexander Tolmer, *Reminiscences of an Adventurous and Chequered Career at Home and at the Antipodes* (2 vols, London: Sampson Low, Marston, Searle, & Rivington, 1882) Vol. II, p. 106. Tolmer quotes Dashwood's police report published in the *Government Gazette*, 16 August 1849.

14   Mr Swaffer, *Register*, 7 May 1926, quoted in the *Observer*, 28 December 1929: 45b.

15   The surname is spelled 'Eastone' is some accounts.

16   Nosworthy & Nosworthy, 1988, p. 16. In one of the best and most interesting of the west coast local histories, Nosworthy and Nosworthy have determined that James Easton married Annie Wilson in New South Wales, and the couple travelled from Sydney to Adelaide on the *Emperor of China*, arriving on 20 September 1848. It seems James Easton settled in the Two Wells district and married again. Just before his death he made enquiries about his first-born son (the letter still exists), but died before a reunion was possible (Pers. Comm., Bill Nosworthy, February 1999).

17   Matthew Moorhouse's Quarterly Report dated 26 July 1849, quoted Tolmer 1882: 2: 108. John Stewart Browne's report notes that the man's name was Meentalta, 'for whom a warrant had already been issued for felony' (GRG 24/6/1849/947, State Records, Adelaide).

18   John B. Hobbs, of Lake Hamilton, in a letter to the *South Australian*, 8 June 1849: 2f claims that Easton's 'wife laid dead on the bed, covered with wounds, and in such a posture as to lead one to suppose that the most barbarous brutality had been committed'. It is also suggests elsewhere that 'Mrs. Easterne [sic] was murdered by a lustful native'. Neville and Margaret Wanklyn, *The early history of the city of Port Lincoln, 1802–1971*, 2nd ed. (Corporation of Port Lincoln, Port Lincoln, 1971), p. 12.

19   Tolmer, 1882, Vol. II, p. 107.

20   GRG 24/6/1849/1404, State Records, Adelaide, p. 8.

21   James Easton left Lake Hamilton after the death of his wife, who is buried in the small cemetery at the northern end of Lake Hamilton. Their son Alfred Easton remained on the west coast all his life, where he worked as a farm labourer. He died in 1910, and is buried in the Poonindie cemetery. His entry in the *Biographical Index of South Australians* reads: 'Alfred Easton. *par*? and Annie. *b*: 1849 Lake Hamilton SA. *d*: 8–11–1910 North Shields SA. *bd* Poonindie SA. *occ*: Labourer. *res*: North Shields. *rel*: C/E. *m*. c.1875 nee HALL *ch*: John Herbert (1876–1964), Annie POWER. Jill Statton, ed. *Biographical Index of South Australians 1836–1885*. 5 vols. (South Australian Genealogy and Heraldry Society, Marden, SA, 1986), Vol. 1, p. 450.

22   Thomas Cooper Horn's name is sometimes given as Horne – apparently he chose to add an 'e' to his name to avoid confusion with W.A. Horn who eventually settled near Streaky Bay. T.C. Horn 'was born in about 1807 at Bramfield, Hertfordshire and arrived in South Australia by 1840' (Nosworthy & Nosworthy, 1988, p. 17). He set up the Kappawanta Run centered around Bramfield of about ninety-one square miles, capable of grazing about 9000 sheep (Nosworthy & Nosworthy, 1988, p. 17). It seems that Horn was not successful with Bramfield and eventually sold out to Price Maurice, for whom Horn later managed the Lake Hamilton Run.

23   The Bramfield Run is not listed in the *Government Gazettes* which list occupational licences issued between 22 December 1842 and 10 February 1848. Nosworthy and Nosworthy speculate that therefore Horn must have taken up the run sometime in 1848, perhaps occupying the land before the licence to stock was actually issued (Nosworthy & Nosworthy, 1988, p. 14). Modern maps show Horn's Lookout in the Hundred of Kappawanta and Lake Horn near Elliston. Waterloo Bay was known as Horn Bay in the 1840s and 1850s.

24   Driver's report is dated 1 July 1849. GRG 24/80/424, State Records, Adelaide.

25   Tolmer mentions the name 'Waterloo Bay' in his memoir (Tolmer, 1882, Vol. II, p. 99) but it is unlikely that he was remembering what the place was actually called in 1849. The name 'Waterloo Bay' carries powerful meanings, in that either way it celebrates a famous moment that helped establish British paramountcy in the nineteenth century. There seems little doubt that the name 'Waterloo Bay' was given to commemorate the rather more famous battle in 1815, not because of a cliff-top skirmish that left three or four people dead. Geoffrey Manning has this to say about the name: 'Prior to June 1865 it [Waterloo Bay] was not shown on maps but during that month the Surveyor-General, G.W. Goyder, and Captain Bloomfield Douglas were in the vicinity in the Government vessel *Flinders*. Therefore, it is probable that it, together with Wellington and Wellesley Points, were so named to celebrate the 50th anniversary of the British victory over Napoleon at Waterloo' (Manning, 1990, p. 329).

26   Tolmer, 1882, Vol. II, p. 99–102. Tolmer records the following revealing detail about how the *male* suspects were restrained: 'Then quickly, at a given signal we simultaneously rushed into the wurlies, each trooper seizing and firmly holding a black-fellow, which is no easy matter in his state of nudity, when he is as slippery as an eel, and is all the while yelling, struggling, and biting as a savage only can. If the captor is experienced, however, by adroitly adopting a peculiar but indescribable knack, the difficulty is much diminished (Tolmer 1882, Vol. II, p. 101). John Wrathall Bull was obviously familiar with this method of restraining Aboriginal suspects, for he alludes discreetly to the practice seemingly pioneered by Major O'Halloran: 'I have the advantage of the use of the diary of Major O'Halloran during the time he was out in the Port Lincoln district to endeavour to *catch and hold* [Bull's emphasis] natives, naked and greasy' (Bull, 1884, p. 298).

27   *Register*, 29 September 1849: 3a. *South Australian*, 2 November 1849, 2f.

28   *South Australian*, 16 November 1849, 2e, *Register*, 17 November 1849, 3b. The so-called hanging tree still stands, near the 80-kilometre road distance marker from Port Lincoln on the eastern side of the Elliston road. Harold Normandale, *To and About Eyre Peninsula* (H. Normandale, Adelaide, 1986), p. 69. The tree still carries what's left of a notice which used to read: 'The Hanging Tree/ Convicted Natives/hung here 1849./Spring cart scaffold/Bodies buried at Port Lincoln').

29   *South Australian Register*, 26 September 1849: 4c.

30   *South Australian*, 11 September 1849, 2f.

31   Matthew Moorhouse argued that if the prisoners had been Europeans they would never have been convicted, in that the prosecution case rested on the testimony of natives. Such evidence had been dismissed in other cases against white men only days previously (and in many other cases) GRG 24/6/1849/1850, State Records, Adelaide.

32   *South Australian Register*, 29 September 1849. See also GRG 24/6/1849/1847, State Records, Adelaide.

33   Charles Driver, letter to Colonial Secretary 11 February 1850, GRG 24/90/424, State Records, Adelaide. See also GRG 24/6/1851/1564, State Records, Adelaide.

34   *Register*, 16 May 1851, *Observer*, 24 May 1851, p. 7, GRG 24/6 1851/1564, State Records, Adelaide. Moorhouse told the court that most natives knew that it was unlawful to kill, but tribal law demanded that strangers might be killed. Moorhouse claimed in court that Maltalta had been charged with Beevor's murder, but Driver mentions that Geharty had arrested him as an accessory in Hamp's murder.

35   GRG/24/90/424, State Records, Adelaide. John Stewart Browne's letter was written c. 12 May 1849.

36   Alexander Tolmer, *Reminiscences of an Adventurous and Chequered Career at Home and at the Antipodes* (London: Sampson Low, Marston, Searle, & Rivington, 1882, 2 vols); 'The Autobiography of Henry Holroyd' D 4108 (L); *I'd rather dig potatoes: Clamor Schürmann and the Aborigines of South Australia*, edited by Edwin A. Schürmann (Lutheran Press, Adelaide 1987); *Recollections: Nathaniel Hailes' adventurous life in South Australia*, edited by Allan L. Peters (Wakefield Press, Kent Town, 1998). Corporal Geharty wrote to Alexander Tolmer, 31 December 1848, about the

state of the district, asserting that '[n]othing has ocured dureing the passed Quarter between the Natives and they Settlers with the exception of the speering of Mr Mortlock's overseer and the late accident at Trial Bay. All the Northwest Settlers Messers Pinkerton Nation Mortlock Vaux Lodwick and Peter has not Been in the Least anoyed During the Quarter they North Settlers has been entiely free from ay atack by they Natives Dureing the Quarter. I think the Native Nirgulta that was comited for trial from hear was about the Greatest anoyance the Northwest Settlers had' (Geharty's spelling, GRG 5, Series 2, #226 of 1848, State Records, Adelaide. Unfortunately no police correspondence survives from 1849).

37 Dr Barbara Wall makes this point very strongly in 'Another look at the Elliston Massacre', *History SA*, no. 122 (January 1994), p. 4.

38 I am grateful to Dr Barbara Wall for biographical information about Congreve and bibliographies of his works.

39 See Stephen Knight, *Continent of Mystery: a Thematic History of Australian Crime Fiction* (Melbourne University Press, Carlton, Vic., 1997) for a general discussion of the taste for sensational and crime fiction in Australia late last century.

40 H.J. Congreve, 'A Reminiscence of Port Lincoln', *Observer*, 14 August 1880, p. 281c.

41 *Register*, 29 September 1849: 2e. See also GRG 24/6/2118, State Records, Adelaide, p. 9.

42 Certainly Stewart's reputation seems to have been well established back in Adelaide. See Charles Sturt's views of Stewart expressed in GRG 24/4/1850/647–48, State Records, Adelaide, which clearly suggests Stewart was suspected of being implicated in 'unhappy collisions' with Indigenous people.

43 *Observer*, 11 September 1880: 428d. The misspelling of Hamp's name is noteworthy, in that Congreve does not name Hamp in his 'A Reminiscence of Port Lincoln'. In other words, Hamp's name is unequivocally linked with the Elliston incident by 1880.

44 *Observer*, 11 September 1880: 428d.

45 The phrase is Henry Kingsley's, from the novel *The Recollections of Geoffry Hamlyn*, taken from Revelations 21:1.

46 Rick Hosking, 'Ellen Liston's "Doctor" and the Elliston Incident', *Southwords: Essays on South Australian Writing*. Edited by Philip Butterss, (Wakefield Press, Kent Town, 1995), pp. 62–84.

47 *Adelaide Observer*, 14 August 1880, p. 283.

48 Ellen Liston, 'Doctor', *Observer*, 17 June 1882, p. 45d.

49 Charter, 1989, p. 61–62. See Henry Price to the Colonial Secretary, GRG 24/6/1851/1559, State Records, Adelaide, for a strongly expressed view that the *servants* had more to fear from attacks than their masters.

50 *A Book of South Australia: Women in the First Hundred Years*, Louise Brown, Beatrix Ch de Crespigny, Mary P. Harris, Kathleen Kyffin Thomas, & Phebe N. Watson, eds., (Rigby, Adelaide, 1936).

51 J.J. Healy, *Literature and the Aborigines in Australia* (University of Queensland Press, St Lucia, 1978), p. xv.

52 Bob Hodge & Vijay Mishra, *Dark Side of the Dream: Australian Literature and the Postcolonial Mind* (Allen & Unwin, North Sydney, 1991).

53 'Interested' claims he first heard the story on either Tallata or Yalluna stations and that '[t]he details were as described by Mr Beviss'. *Observer*, 20 March 1926, p. 16c.

54 E.W. Parish, *The Real West Coast: A New Picture of a Rumour-Damaged Country* (W.K. Thomas, Adelaide, 1906), p. 8.

55 'A Fine Record: Inspector Clode's Retirement', *Register*, 20 July 1915, p. 11b. Clode argued that the Elliston locality should be called the Hundred of Hamp.

56 John Dow, 'Waterloo Bay', *Register*, 24 February 1926, p. 8c.

57 *Observer*, 13 March 1926, p. 14c.

58 See Manning, 1990, p. 106.

59 Pers. Comm. Bill Nosworthy, 1998. See Nosworthy & Nosworthy, 1988, p. 16.

60 P. Hosking, *The Official Civic Record of South Australia: Centenary Year 1936* (Universal Publicity Company, Adelaide, 1936), p. 558.

61 J.F. O'Dea, *Elliston: A brief outline of the history of this area of Eyre Peninsula* (Elliston?: the Author, n.d.), p. 1.

62 O'Dea, n.d., p. 2.

63 *Observer*, 9 December 1905, p. 28.

64 D.R. Myer, 'Reminiscences of a Pioneer, born 1846', typescript, PRG 458/7/7. This typescript has a note 'Appeared in weekly instalments in the *Port Lincoln Times*, 22 May–3 July 1931'.

65 N.A. Richardson, 'Waterloo Bay Massacre', *Register* 24 October 1929, p. 6. If this was the story that Hamp often told, then at least one detail is inaccurate. The suspects for his father's murder were never hanged: however, two men were convicted on Captain Beevor's murder and hanged at Taunto, 80 kilometres from Port Lincoln.

66 Max Fatchen, 'Massacre of the Aborigines', *Advertiser*, 11 April 1970, p. 17.

67 Ibid.

68 'Waterloo Bay Massacre', *Advertiser*, 15 October 1937, p. 3a.

69 PRG 458/6, State Records, Adelaide.

70 GRG 24/6/1848/1127, State Records, Adelaide, dated 17 July 1848.

71 GRG 24/6/1848/1152, State Records, Adelaide, dated 26 July 1848; GRG 24/6/1848/1156, State Records, Adelaide.

72 GRG 24/6/1848/1127, State Records, Adelaide, dated 17 July 1848.

73 Henry Holroyd, 'South Australian Pioneer. His Autobiography'. Written in 1902 and held in the Mortlock Library: D.4108/7(L), p. 27.

74 Quoted in *News*, 2 April 1970, p. 13.

75 Thompson 1969, p. 176–8.

76 Interview by Neil Thompson with Mr and Mrs Roche at their home at 10 Park St, Glandore, 17 September 1965, quoted in Thompson & Thompson 1988, p. 23.

77 GRG 24/6/1849/2118, State Records, Adelaide, p. 6. Judge Cooper notes that the 'confessions given by prisoners to Geharty cannot be relied on'.

78 GRG 24/6/1849/1847, State Records, Adelaide.

79 *Observer*, 24 April 1926, p. 60.

80 *Advertiser*, 4 August 1932, p. 10i. Reminiscences of M.S.W. Kenny.

81 Thompson & Thompson, 1988, p. 23.

82 GRG 24/6/1848/1127, State Records, Adelaide, p. 3.

83 GRG 24/6/1848/1152, State Records, Adelaide, p. 3.

84 GRG 24/6/1848/1156, State Records, Adelaide, p. 4.

85 *Register*, 29 September 1849, p. 2e.

86 Ibid., p. 3a.

87 See also the *Register*, 29 September 1849, pp. 2e–3a for a detailed account of the trial.

88 This evidence later helped to save the suspects from the gallows: at no stage did the prosecution establish that Korti Warri was in fact Weepra Spring where Hamp lived.

89 Similarly the prosecution could not establish that Tommy and John Hamp were one and the same.

90 GRG 24/6/1849/2118, State Records, Adelaide, pp. 6–7, dated 20 November 1849. This is remarkable evidence. Judge Cooper argued that it could not be used to clearly identify 'Tommy' as John Hamp, an argument which saved Mingulta and Mangalta from hanging. The evidence also gives Korti Warri (or Warrie) as the Wirangu (?) name for Weepra Spring on Stoney Point, Lake Newland although as Cooper notes we can not be sure that the witness was describing what the Europeans knew as Weepra Spring or Stoney Point.

91 GRG 24/6/1849/2118, State Records, Adelaide, p. 8.

92 GRG 24/6/1849/2118, State Records, Adelaide, p. 9.

93 *South Australian*, 21 July 1848, p. 2a.

94   Tolmer 1882, Vol. II, p. 105.

95   GRG 24/6/1851/1744, State Records, Adelaide.

96   Clamor Schürmann, *I'd Rather Dig Potatoes*, p. 154. (Lutheran Publishing House, Adelaide, 1987).

97   The writer probably means William Hosken, of Waranda Well (Faull 1988, p. 39) and not some long-forgotten relative of one of the authors. His properties included Chillundie, Chilperundie and Muddamuckla: he also had a lease on St Peter's Island off Ceduna.

98   *Register*, 29 September 1849, p. 2e.

99   The letters of P.J. Baillie. PRG 458/6.

100 Lisa Baker, *Calca 1885–1991: History of Calca* (Calca Book Committee, Calca, 1991), p. 19. See also Neil Thompson & Val Thompson, *The Streaky Bay: A History of the Streaky Bay District* (The Streaky Bay District Council, Streaky Bay, 1988), p. 78.

101 Basil Fuller, *Nullarbor Lifelines* (Rigby, Adelaide, 1977), p. 185.

102 J.D. Somerville, *The Port Lincoln Times Centenary History of the early Days of Eyre Peninsula*. Held in the Mortlock Library (Z 994.2/b). See the entries beginning on 18 September 1936, running through to 27 November 1936. His views, like those of Rodney Cockburn's, are occasionally defensively belligerent on the subject: '[t]he white men, now and again, in self defence and in attempting to arrest raiders, may have shot down a few raiders', quoted in *Across the Bar to Waterloo Bay: Elliston 1878–1978*, p. 5.

103 P.J. Baillie, 'The Waterloo Bay Story', *Chronicle*, 3 December 1971, p. 43.

104 Charter, 1989, p. 65.

105 A.T. Saunders, 'Waterloo Bay', *Register*, 29 March 1926, p. 13e.

106 Ellen Liston, 'Doctor', in *Pioneers: Stories by Ellen Liston*. Compiled by E.A. Harwood (The Hassell Press, Adelaide, 1936), p. 58.

107 Pat Sumerling, 'The myth of the Elliston Massacre', *History SA*, No. 120, 1995, pp. 4–5.

108 *News*, 7 April 1979, p. 20.

109 Max Fatchen, *Advertiser*, Wednesday 25 March 1970, p. 17.

110 *News*, 18 February 1970, p. 2.

111 'Plan to recall "massacre",' *Advertiser*, 24 March 1970, p. 11.

112 Jeff Turner, 'What did Happen at Waterloo Bay?' *News*, 2 April 1970, pp. 12–13.

113 Norman Ford, 'Massacre legend', *Advertiser*, 30 March 1970, p. 2.

114 Laurie Bryan, 'Massacre incident', *Advertiser*, 3 April 1970, p. 2. The noun in the headline is worth a comment: Ford's letter describes a 'legend', Bryan's an 'incident'. The contentious nature of the subject is clearly manifested. The printing of the letter with a number of spelling errors included is also a not-so-subtle indication of the attitudes of the *Advertiser* staff.

115 Pat Sumerling, 'The myth of the Elliston massacre: The value of memory,' *History SA: Newsletter of the Historical Society of SA* No. 120 (1995), p. 4.

116 Perhaps the detail of the chains has been taken from stories still told about James Brown by Ngarrindjeri people from the Coorong and the South East. The same story has been collected from two members of the Ngarrindjeri community about Brown chaining his victims to the rock wall of a cave and leaving them to die when the tide came in (Pers. Comm. at the opening of the David Unaipon Centre at the University of South Australia, 1996).

117 Pers. Comm., 1994.

118 The plaque on Hamp's grave reads: 'JOHN HAMP/KILLED BY THE NATIVES NEAR THIS SPOT/MAY 3RD 1848/ERECTED IN 1971 BY/THE PT LINCOLN CALEDONIAN SOCIETY/P.J. BAILLIE CHIEF'.

119 J.J. Healy, *Literature and the Aborigine in Australia*, 2nd ed. (University of Queensland Press, St Lucia, 1989), p. xv.

THE LEGEND OF JAMES BROWN

1 Rodney Cockburn, *Pastoral Pioneers of South Australia*, Vol. I (Lynton Publications, Adelaide, 1974, facsimile of the original by Publishers Limited, Adelaide, 1925–27), p. 140. What the passage glosses over is that these institutions were established after Brown's death and at the instigation of his wife.

2 Ibid., pp. 140–41.

3 Ibid., p. 141.

4 J.G. Hastings, *The History of the Coorong, from the original by J.G. Hastings 'Glengowan' Meningie, 20.12.1944*, Typescript, Mortlock Library, Adelaide.

5 Tom McCourt & Hans Mincham, *The Coorong and Lakes of the Lower Murray* (The Beachport Branch of the National Trust, Gillingham Printers, Adelaide, 1987), pp. 92–3.

6 Ibid.

7 Philip Clarke and Steven Hemming, personal communication. We have been unable to locate the audio recording of the interview. The details here come from Philip Clarke's field notes. Steven Hemming's recollections broadly corroborate the account.

8 McCourt & Mincham, pp. 92–3.

9 Education Department of South Australia, *The Ngarrindjeri People: Aboriginal People of the River Murray, Lakes and Coorong. An Aboriginal Studies Course for Secondary Students in Years 8–10* (Education Department of South Australia, Publications Branch, Adelaide, 1990), pp. 139–40.

10 Ibid., p. 139.

11 This version of the story is told by George Trevorrow. In 1987, George Trevorrow was instrumental in establishing the Camp Coorong Race Relations and Cultural Education Centre, near Meningie, about 320 kilometres south-east of Adelaide. At this time he was employed by the South Australian Education Department as regional co-ordinator of Aboriginal Education Workers. See Steven Hemming, 'Camp Coorong – Combining Race Relations and Cultural Education', *Social Alternatives*, Vol. 12, no. 1, April 1993, pp. 37–40.

12 Ibid., p. 140.

13 Protector of Aborigines, Report to the Chief Secretary, 6 March 1849, GRG 24/6/457/1849, State Records, Adelaide.

14 Letter of Captain G.V. Butler to C.H. Bagot, 14 April 1849, D. 3746/2 (L), Mortlock Library, Adelaide; Protector of Aborigines, Report to the Chief Secretary, 6 March 1849, GRG 24/6/457/1849, State Records, Adelaide.

15 Protector of Aborigines, Report to the Chief Secretary, 6 March 1849, GRG 24/6/457/1849, State Records, Adelaide.

16 Protector's Report, 23 October 1849, in *South Australian Government Gazette*, 1 November 1849, pp. 498–9.

17 Advocate General to Chief Secretary, 26 July 1849, GRG 24/6/1388/1849, State Records, Adelaide.

18 Letter of Captain G.V. Butler to C.H. Bagot, 21 May 1849, D. 3746/3 (L), Mortlock Library, Adelaide.

19 *South Australian Register*, 13 June 1849.

20 Ibid., 20 June 1849.

21 Advocate General to Chief Secretary, 26 July 1849, GRG 24/6/1388/1849, State Records, Adelaide.

22 *South Australian Register*, 12 & 29 September 1849.

23 Ibid., 27 November 1849.

24 Robert Foster, The Bunganditj: European Invasion and the Economic Basis of Social Collapse, MA thesis, University of Adelaide, pp. 134–8.

25 Christina Smith, Diary, pp. 25–6, PRG 144, Mortlock Library, Adelaide.

26 Ibid.

27 Christina Smith, *The Booandik Tribe of South Australian Aborigines* (Government Printer, Adelaide, 1880), pp. 60–2.
28 Ibid., p. 62.
29 Ibid.
30 Foster, Appendix III.
31 Ibid, pp. 110–11.
32 Ibid., Appendix III; the alleged killing of eight Aborigines in May 1844 was reported by Sergeant Major Alford, Chief Secretary's Office, Inward Correspondence, GRG 24/6/116/1845, State Records, Adelaide.
33 *Criminal Record Books, 1836–1900*, Supreme Court of South Australia, Adelaide.
34 Chief Secretary's Office, Inward Correspondence, GRG 24/6/116/1845, State Records, Adelaide.
35 Ibid.
36 Smith, p. 26.
37 Protector's Report, 23 October 1849, in *South Australian Government Gazette*, 1 November 1849, pp. 498–9.
38 Simpson Newland, *Paving the Way, a Romance of the Australian Bush* (Moroak, Encounter Bay, South Australia, 1982, Facsimile of the 1893 edition), p. v. Newland's fictionalisation of actual events is evident in the episode that commences the novel, the shipwreck of the *Mary*. This is a thinly disguised account of the shipwreck of the *Maria*, and the killing of the survivors by Aborigines.
39 Cockburn, Vol. 1, p. 96; Simpson Newland, 'Some Aborigines I Have Known', *Proceedings of the Royal Geographical Society of Australasia, South Australian Branch*, Vol. 2, 1894–95, pp. 1–15.
40 Ibid, p. 130.
41 Ibid.
42 Ibid., p. 132.
43 Ibid., p. 133.
44 Ibid., p. 161.
45 In this year, four men, including Brown, were charged with murder and another was charged with rape. All the charges were either dismissed, or, as in Brown's case, dropped. *Criminal Record Book, 1849*, Supreme Court of South Australia, Adelaide.
46 Newland, p. 132.
47 *South Australian Register*, 8 September 1849.
48 *South Australian Parliamentary Debates*, Vol. 1, 7 September 1939, p. 846.
49 Elma J. Smith, *History of Kingston* (Country Women's Association, Kingston, 1950), p. 1.
50 Account by Verne McLaren in Jessie Banks, *Kingston Flashbacks* (Ladies' Auxiliary of Kingston District Soldiers' Memorial Hospital, Kingston, 1970), pp. 7–8.
51 Ibid.
52 Barry Durman, *A History of 'The Bakers Range Settlement'* (Lucindale Centenary Publication, Naracoorte, 1978), pp. 8–9.
53 Ibid.
54 Ibid.
55 David Roberts, 'Bells Falls Massacre and Bathurst's History of Violence: Local Tradition and Australian Historiography', *Australian Historical Studies*, Vol. 26, no. 105, October 1995, p. 627.
56 C. Healy, *From the Ruins of Colonialism* (Cambridge University Press, Cambridge, 1997), p. 123.

FATAL COLLISIONS IN THE FLINDERS RANGES

1 See for example Robert Bruce, *Reminiscences of an Old Squatter* (W.K. Thomas, Adelaide, 1902), p. 165. Bruce's view about the number of deaths from inter-racial conflict in the Flinders is reinforced by a recent study which asserts that 'trouble between natives and settlers was never as bad in the Flinders Ranges as it was on Eyre Peninsula or along the Murray. Nonetheless, in the

late 1840s and then in the 1850s a dozen or more European men were killed and probably a score or more Aboriginals'. (*The Flinders Ranges: An Aboriginal View*, Christine Davis, Clifford Coulthard and Desmond Coulthard (Eds.), (Aboriginal Heritage Branch, Department of Environment and Planning, Adelaide, 1980), p. 11.

2   GRG 24/6/1852/1146. Document #1 in the file. State Records, Adelaide.

3   Ibid.

4   Ibid.

5   Ibid.

6   *Register*, 20 April 1852, 3d. *Register*, 22 November 1852, p. 3e, records that *'Jemmy*, (a native) – Feloniously did kill and murder Robert Robertson, on the 14th of March, 1852, at Youngoona. Remanded from August last'.

7   GRG 24/6/1852/1513. State Records, Adelaide.

8   Ibid.

9   Ibid.

10   GRG 24/6/1852/1733. State Records, Adelaide.

11   GRG 24/6/1852/1793. State Records, Adelaide.

12   Ibid. State Records, Adelaide.

13   GRG 24/6/1854/1146. State Records, Adelaide.

14   *Observer*, 3 July 1852, p. 6bcd

15   Although Moorhouse does not make it clear, it may be that the 'Lake Torrens blacks' were in the vicinity of Aroona on their way to or from the famous ochre mines, one of which was on the Aroona lease, the other at Bookartoo, near Parachilna. They may have been either Banggarla, Kuyani or even Kokotha people.

16   *Observer*, 10 April 1852, p. 5e.

17   *Register*, 21 April 1852, p. 2e and 3a, reprinted with some small corrections in the *Observer*, 24 April 1852, p. 5e. The editorial goes on to demonstrate that it cost £41/15/- to send Dr Matthew Moorhouse, the Protector of Aborigines and a police contingent north to enquire into the reported murder of a native near Mount Arden, whereas the expense of maintaining the police station at Mount Remarkable for the three months it was closed (15 February–15 April 1852) was only £24/14/6, including wages of £3 for a Native Constable.

18   It was only Moorhouse's direct intervention in the case that led to the arrest, conviction and execution of Thomas Donnelly, the only white man to be hanged for killing an Indigenous Australian in South Australia in the nineteenth century. Donnelly was hanged in 1846, and it is clear that both Moorhouse's diligence and the example of Donnelly encouraged those who had killed Aboriginal people to do their best to keep their activities from the attention of the law. See Dewdney's note about another employee on Aroona, Johnny Bose who 'would have if at home caught, got into trouble for shooting an impudent Black, but then in his wisdom kept out of the way until matters quietened (Dewdney, 1924?, pp. 9–10).

19   *Advertiser*, 19 May 1928, p. 11e. The identical article with differing headlines and subheadings appeared in the *Register*, 19 May 1928, p. 16g.

20   An handwritten version of Hayward's 'Reminiscences' can be found in the Mortlock Library of South Australiana, PRG 395, Papers of J.F. Hayward. 'Incidents of my Australian Life, 1846 to 1856' (with occasional references to later dates).

21   Buchanan, Alexander, *Diary of a Journal Overland from Sydney to Adelaide with Sheep. July-December, 1839. By A Pioneer of 1839. The Royal Geographic Society of Australasia (SA Branch)*, Vol. 24, 1923.

22   In passing, the *Advertiser* gave the piece the byline 'Early Days in the North. Reminiscences of a Pastoral Pioneer', with the sub-headings 'Thieving Native Tribes'. 'Heavy Losses'. 'The Aroona Run'. and 'Prosperous Times'. The *Register* used the byline 'Farthest Out Station. Pioneer Narrates Experiences. Natives Seriously Hindered Development', with the sub-headings 'Exasperating Difficulties'. 'Punishment of Marauders'. 'Unauthorized Revenge'. 'Interesting Record'. Obviously the *Register* editor had a slightly more sensitive understanding of the political

significance of Hayward's 'Reminiscences', hinting at behaviour that might have been 'unauthorized' or illegal.

23 *Advertiser*, 19 May 1928, p. 11e.
24 Hayward's complicity in widespread violence against the Yuras has been noted by a number of commentators (Mincham, 1964; Brock, 1986 and Mattingley 1986, to name but three).
25 Hayward, 1929, p. 92.
26 Ibid., p. 131.
27 Ibid., p. 103.
28 *Advertiser*, 31 March 1925, p. 14f carries an obituary for Mrs Hayward.
29 Hayward, 1929, p. 103.
30 Ibid., p. 107.
31 Ibid., p. 137–40.
32 *Observer*, 10 April 1852, p. 5e.
33 PRG 395, The Papers of J.F. Hayward.
34 Ibid., p. 103–4.
35 Ibid., p. 131.
36 Ibid., p. 140.
37 Ibid., p. 137–42.
38 Ibid., p. 142.
39 By 1852 in partnership with his brother Ellar, 'Big' John McKinlay had established a run, Owienagan, now called Hannigan's Gap, under Patawarta Hill to the north of Hayward's Aroona lease. At the time Owienagan must have been the most northerly run in South Australia. McKinlay was later to achieve nation-wide fame for his exploits in the search for the survivors of the Burke and Wills expedition. In 1861 he was the first European to lead a team from the south to the north coast of Australia and successfully return, and is also remembered for his 'discoveries' in the Northern Territory. See Kim Lockwood, *Big John: The Extraordinary Adventures of John McKinlay 1819–1872* (State Library of Victoria, Melbourne).
40 Geoffrey Manning notes that 'Hayward Creek in the North Flinders Ranges was named by John McKinlay on 3 January 1862' (Manning, 1990, p. 145), clearly suggesting that the two men were close.
41 J.B. Bull *Reminiscences 1835–94*, SA Archives 950, p. 73.
42 John Bowyer Bull was born in England in 1834, arrived in South Australia in 1838, ran away from home, went to the Diggings in Victoria and then returned to South Australia in 1855 (Mincham, 1964, p. 104).
43 Original spelling, Bull 1894?, p. 75.
44 At the back of the second volume of John Bowyer Bull's diary held in the Mortlock Library are notes in his father's hand.
45 John Wrathall Bull, *Early Experiences of Life in South Australia, and An Extended Colonial History* (E.S. Wigg & Sons, Adelaide, 1884), p. 98. It is worth noting that in his *Pastoral Pioneers of South Australia* Cockburn makes no reference to the Richardson murder and its aftermath other than to quote this paragraph from J.W. Bull without comment (Cockburn, 1927, p. 109).
46 'Reminiscences Past (?) to Present by Richard Dewdney', Mortlock Library of South Australiana (D 7436(L)). Dewdney's obituary can be found in the *Register* 26 March 1924, p. 10, where he is described as the 'Pastoralist's Friend'. Dewdney had arrived in the colony in 1860 on the *Orient*, and had joined his brother on Orraparina [*sic*]. In 1862 he took up a job for George and Frank Marchant on Arkaba where he remained until the drought of 1864–5. Later he managed the Yardea Run in the Gawler Ranges for Acraman, Main, Lindsay and Co., the Paney Run, Boolcomatta Station, the Wonoka Run, among others.
47 Dewdney, 1924?, pp. 9–10.
48 *Advertiser*, 31 March 1925, p. 14f.
49 *Observer*, 13 April 1912, p. 49a.

50 Letter from George Dashwood, Collector of Customs, to the Colonial Secretary, 23 January 1855. GRG 24/6/1855/363. State Records, Adelaide.

51 Bruce, 1902, p. 89.

52 Ibid., p. 201.

53 Ibid., p. 201.

54 Bruce was obviously more taken with Hayward as a model for the ideal squatter than he was with his employer Frank Marchant. The Marchant brothers seem not to have taken such extreme measures against the Yuras as Hayward, although Jessop records this ambivalent series of observations about them formed from a meeting when Bruce was in Frank Marchant's employ: 'From the dangers which the Marchants encountered, when they first came into this part of the country, they have no very great affection for the natives. It may be natural to mistrust and mislike them, on account of the opposition which they offered to the settlement of the white invader, but, poor wretches, they would he held in greater contempt if they did not show fight. Right-down pluck always commands admiration, and, however we may disguise it under approbrious terms, the defence of his inheritance, though slighted and insulted as ferocious hostility, ought to be considered as the finest opportunity the black man has for showing the stuff that is in him. . . . It is a melancholy thing to find that these miserable creatures cannot be allowed to die out in their own way, without hurrying them out of the land with rifles' (Jessop, 1862, Vol. 2, pp. 166–7). It is tempting to assume that Jessop heard stories about the Marchants and their employees and their 'campaigns' against the Yura – he finishes his discussion of the consequences of 'white invasion' with a remark I take to be ironic: 'Better leave these things [standing up for black against white] to men who know all about the treachery, cruelty, and craftiness of these blood-thirsty villains' (Jessop, p. 167). His remark does not make it clear who are the villains.

55 Robert Bruce, *Reminiscences of an Old Squatter* (W.K. Thomas and Co., Adelaide, 1902), p. 108.

56 Robert Bruce's spelling of the name of the hut in question as 'Younganna' is of some interest. He suggests that the word means 'the Lake Hope cockatoo' *Cacatua sanguinea*, the ubiquitous little corella of the Flinders, much more common now than it was in the 1850s. Bruce says that 'Younganna' is the Yura Ngawarla name for the bird. Dr Susan Hosking has suggested that Bruce inadvertently may be alluding to a Yura Dreaming story, a Nugunu version of which was collected by the Ngarrindjeri writer David Unaipon. Unaipon includes a 'native legend' about 'Youn Goona,' a Dreaming hero in his *Native Legends* (Adelaide: Aborigines' Friends Association, [1929]). Given that he collected stories from all around South Australia, it may be that his 'legend' preserves in vestigial form a Yura Dreaming. The discovery of the similarity in names makes one aware of the survival of fragments of information about Indigenous cosmology and epistemology. See Susan Hosking, 'David Unaipon – His Story', in *Southwords: Essays on South Australian Writing*, edited by Philip Butterss (Wakefield Press, Adelaide, 1995), p. 98.

57 Rodney Cockburn, *Pastoral Pioneers of South Australia*, [Facsimile ed.] 2 Volumes, indexed by A. Dorothy Aldersey (Publishers Limited, Adelaide, 1925–27) Vol. 2, p. 79.

58 Simpson Newland, 'Preface', *Paving the Way: A Romance of the Australian Bush* (Gay & Bird, London, 1893).

59 Contributors named include: Environment and Natural Resources, State Heritage Branch, ETSA, the South Australian Museum, Mines and Energy South Australia, South Australian Tourist Commission, the Geography departments of both Adelaide and Flinders Universities, the Department of Human and Environmental Science of the University of South Australia, Flinders Ranges and Outback South Australia Tourism, Recreation SA, the Mortlock Library of South Australiana, local government officers and landholders. Sponsorship by Pasminco Metals–BHAS is also gratefully acknowledged (p. ii).

60 Some of the information available in *Explore the Flinders Ranges* was formerly available in a series of pamphlets published before 1996, one of which is titled *Hayward's Huts* and features a couple of walks in and around the Aroona Valley.

61 Geoffrey Manning records the following about Hayward: "Unique in the nomenclature of the Flinders Ranges, Hayward's name appears four times on the map within 3 km for prominent features in the Heysen Range. Directly south-west from the ruins of his old Aroona station stands Mount Hayward (865 metres), the highest in the Heysen Range; south of it, each successively 11 metres lower, are South Mount Hayward and False Mount Hayward. Finally, southern-most, there is the bold, precipitous, broad-faced Hayward Bluff which was apparently the first to be named for it alone was marked on J.B. Austin's map in 1863. Hayward Creek in the North Flinders Ranges was named by John McKinlay on 3 January 1862. J.F. Hayward held the Aroona Run (lease no. 83 of July 1851)' (Geoffrey Manning, *Manning's Place Names of South Australia*, The Author, Adelaide, 1990), p. 145.

62 Sue Barker, Murray McCaskill & Brian Ward, *Explore the Flinders Ranges* (Royal Geographical Society of Australasia, South Australian Branch, Adelaide, 1996) p. 29.

63 Bruce's novel *Benbonuna* ends with the following paragraph: 'And now, to conclude. Mr Ashby's station has for years been cut up into farmers' holdings, the owners of which, when they clamoured for its resumption, were wont to declare that 'rain followed the plough'; now they might own with sorrow that, were the letter 'u' substituted for 'a' in rain, then the sentence, thus slightly altered, would be only too applicable to the introduction of the plough to Benbonuna'. Evidence of nostalgia for a pastoral 'golden age' emerged very early, it seems.

64 Both Chris Healy and Rob Foster have argued that *local* histories are characteristically more revealing about levels of violence on the frontier than 'national' histories. In passing I note that guidebooks and tourist publications about nationally recognised eidetic icons like the Flinders Ranges are relatively *less* likely to stress high levels of frontier violence, more likely to reflect the prevailing national(ist) ideologies about the past which Prime Minister Howard has been keen to promulgate in his attacks on 'black armband' histories.

65 Ann Clancy, *The Wild Colonial Girl* (Pan Macmillan, Sydney, 1996).

66 Clancy, 1996, p. 89.

67 Ibid., p. 224.

68 Ibid., p. 248.

LOGIC'S UNEXPECTED CELEBRITY

1 *Adelaide Observer*, 6 April 1878.

2 Ibid.

3 Ibid., 4 May 1878.

4 Ibid.

5 Ibid., 27 July 1878.

6 Ibid., 4 May 1878.

7 Ibid.

8 Ibid.

9 Ibid.

10 Ibid.

11 Police Department, Police Commissioner's Office Correspondence Files, 18 July 1878 & 13 August 1878, GRG 5/2/1878/846. State Records, Adelaide.

12 *Adelaide Observer*, 25 December 1880.

13 Police Department, Beltana Station Journal, 27 October 1880–28 December 1880, GRG 5/300/2. State Records, Adelaide.

14 *Australian Dictionary of Biography* (ADB), (Melbourne University Press, Melbourne, 1966–[2000]), Vol. 3, 1851–1890, pp. 199–200.

15 *Adelaide Observer*, 26 February 1881.

16 ADB, Vol. 3, pp. 35–36.

17   *South Australian Government Gazette*, 10 February, 1881, p. 417; Supreme Court of South Australia, *Letterbooks of the Master's Office*, 1879–80.

18   J. Boucaut, *Criminal Notebook*, 22 February 1881. Supreme Court of South Australia.

19   Ibid.

20   Ibid.

21   Ibid.

22   Ibid.

23   Ibid.

24   Supreme Court of South Australia, *Criminal Sittings Record Book 1880–1881*, 22 February 1881, p. 351.

25   Department of Correctional Services, *Control Register of Prisoners* (Yatala Labour Prison), 1881, p. 470. GRG 54/90. State Records, Adelaide.

26   Ibid.

27   *Adelaide Observer*, 30 June 1860.

28   Ibid., 17 February 1883.

29   Correspondence files of the Sheriff's Office, GRG 54/1/1885/183, 13 January 1882. State Records, Adelaide.

30   GRG 24/1/1885/2233, 8 October 1885. State Records. Adelaide.

31   Statement of Guard R.W. Barrien, GRG 54/1/1885/253. State Records, Adelaide.

32   Ibid.

33   Ibid.

34   Ibid.

35   Ibid.

36   Ibid., Statement of Acting Chief Guard H. Barrien.

37   *Advertiser*, 21 December 1885.

38   *Adelaide Observer*, 24 October 1885.

39   *The Pictorial Australian*, November 1886.

40   *Adelaide Observer*, 15 December 1885.

41   Ibid., 24 October 1885.

42   *Advertiser*, 5 November 1885.

43   Beltana Station Journal, 16 & 17 November 1885. GRG 5/300/2. State Records, Adelaide.

44   *Advertiser*, 25 November 1885.

45   Ibid., 7 December 1885.

46   Ibid.

47   Ibid.

48   Ibid., 21 December 1885.

49   Ibid.

50   Ibid., 7 December 1885.

51   Ibid., 21 December 1885.

52   *Port Augusta Dispatch*, 9 December 1885.

53   *Advertiser*, 11 December 1885.

54   *Port Augusta Dispatch*, 14 December 1885.

55   *Advertiser*, 12 December 1885.

56   *Port Augusta Dispatch*, 14 December 1885.

57   *Advertiser*, 21 December 1885.

58   *Port Augusta Dispatch*, 18 December 1885.

59   *Adelaide Observer*, 14 December 1885.

60   Ibid., 19 December 1885.

61   Ibid.

62   *Advertiser*, 15 December 1885.

63   Ibid.

64   Ibid.
65   Ibid.
66   Ibid.
67   Ibid.
68   *Adelaide Observer*, 19 December 1885.
69   GRG 24/1/1885/2233. State Records, Adelaide.
70   *South Australian Parliamentary Debates*, 11 December 1885, p. 1909.
71   R. Foster, An Imaginary Dominion: The Representation and Treatment of Aborigines in South Australia, 1834–1911, PhD Thesis, University of Adelaide, 1993, pp. 147–74.
72   Ibid., pp. 250–53.
73   G. Taplin, *The Narrinyeri, their Manners and Customs* (Government Printers, Adelaide, 1873).
74   Protector's Report, 10 August 1874, *South Australian Government Gazette*, 18 March 1875, p. 510.
75   S. Gason, *The Dieyerie Tribe of Australian Aborigines; their Manners and Customs* (Government Printers, Adelaide, 1874); J. Smith, *The Booandik Tribe of South Australian Aborigines* (Government Printers, Adelaide, 1880).
76   *South Australian Register*, 30 May 1885.
77   *Adelaide Observer*, 6 June 1885.
78   For South Australia's Jubilee Exhibition see *The Lantern*, 30 October 1886, p. 22; *Adelaide Observer*, 10 September 1887. For South Australia's contribution to intercolonial and international exhibitions see *Adelaide Observer*, 24 July 1886; L. Kinney & Z. Celik, 'Ethnography and Exhibitionism at the Expositions Universalles', *Assemblage*, 13 (December 1990), pp. 35–36; P. Jones, 'Collections and Curators: South Australian Museum Anthropology from the 1860s to the 1920s', *Journal of the Historical Society of South Australia*, no. 16, 1988, p. 93.
79   *The Pictorial Australian*, January 1886.
80   Ibid.
81   Ibid.
82   *Northern Argus*, 15 December 1885.
83   *South Australian Register*, 16 December 1885.
84   GRG 24/1/1885/2687. State Records, Adelaide.
85   *Adelaide Observer*, 16 January 1886; *Port Augusta Dispatch*, 15 January 1886.
86   *Adelaide Observer*, 30 January 1886.
87   Aborigines Department, Index to Correspondence, GRG 52/2/1/1886/31. State Records, Adelaide.
88   H. Tolcher, *Drought or Deluge* (Melbourne University Press, Melbourne, 1986), p. 144.
89   *Adelaide Observer*, 22 February 1890; *South Australian Register*, 3 January 1890, 23 January 1890.
90   *Adelaide Observer*, 20 February 1890.
91   Ibid., 22 January 1890.
92   Ibid., 14 December 1889.
93   Tolcher, p. 144.
94   *Adelaide Observer*, 9 January 1904.
95   Ibid., 16 July 1910.
96   A. Grant, *Camel, Train and Aeroplane* (Adelaide, 1981), pp. 97–98.
97   *Adelaide Observer*, 8 September 1928.
98   *Adelaide Chronicle*, 26 August 1937.

EPILOGUE: UNSETTLING THE PAST

1   B. Attwood, 'Mabo, Australia and the End of History', in Bain Attwood (ed.), *In the Age of Mabo* (Allen & Unwin, St. Leonards, 1996), p. 107.
2   Ibid., p. 106.
3   Cited in Attwood, 1996, p. 107.

INDEX

■

COLONIALISM AND ITS AFTERMATH

A HISTORY OF ABORIGINAL SOUTH AUSTRALIA

Edited by Peggy Brock and Tom Gara

The state of South Australia was a British imperial construct, its borders determined by three straight lines, with no reference to the Aboriginal presence.

The colonial process in South Australia began decades before formal annexation with unregulated interactions between coastal Aboriginal people and European sealers and whalers.

Despite catastrophic interventions in the lives of Aboriginal people during and following colonisation, many communities retain strong identities and cultural and linguistic knowledge, rooted in a deep connection to the land.

Colonialism and its Aftermath traces the ongoing impact of colonialism on Aboriginal individuals, communities and cultures, the disruptions and displacements it has caused, and Aboriginal responses to these challenges.

Contributors:
Diane Bell, Peggy Brock, Jennifer Caruso, Deane Fergie, Robert Foster, Mary-Anne Gale, Tom Gara, Des Hartman, Luise Hercus, Rani Kerin, Skye Krichauff, Christine Lockwood, Rod Lucas, Ingereth Macfarlane, Paul Monaghan, Amanda Nettelbeck, Chris Nobbs, Carol Pybus, Lester-Irabinna Rigney, Tikari Rigney and Phyllis Williams

For more information visit www.wakefieldpress.com.au

ALICE SPRINGS

FROM SINGING WIRE TO ICONIC OUTBACK TOWN

Stuart Traynor

In 1870 a colonial government, on the brink of collapse, made an audacious move. South Australia's squabbling politicians briefly put aside their differences and took the bold decision to run an iron wire to the middle of nowhere and beyond. Stringing the Overland Telegraph Line across the silent heart of the continent was a momentous event in the country's history. It connected Adelaide to a global network of cables and wire: those travelling up and down the track through central Australia were seldom out of earshot of its hum. Alice Springs was its most important repeater station.

Alice Springs: From singing wire to iconic outback town is the result of eight years of meticulous research unravelling the early history of central Australia's first white settlement. It contains information, never previously published, about that little outpost – a significant heritage site – and how an iconic town was born nearby, during a goldrush that made few people rich. It is a tale of the country's heart and some of its most remarkable but little-known characters, and of children torn between two cultures living at the telegraph station after the morse keys stopped clicking in 1932; children under the shadow of the most controversial piece of legislation in Australia's history. Central Australia has a black history.

Alice Springs is no longer the small, outback community romanticised in Nevil Shute's novel *A Town like Alice*. But its people, black and white, are still living on the line.

Winner of the 2017 Chief Minister's Northern Territory History Book Award

For more information visit www.wakefieldpress.com.au

IN THE NAME OF THE LAW

*WILLIAM WILLSHIRE AND THE POLICING OF THE
AUSTRALIAN FRONTIER*

Amanda Nettelbeck and Robert Foster

Mounted Constable William Willshire commanded a corps of Native Police in Central Australia during the 1880s. Notorious for the violence of his patrols, he was eventually tried in 1891 for the murder of two Aboriginal men, and was posted to an even more remote frontier in the Top End. During his time in the Territory, Willshire wrote of his experiences in several extraordinary memoirs. Part murder mystery and part courtroom drama, his story illuminates unfolding issues of race and nationalism in colonial Australia on the eve of Federation.

For more information visit www.wakefieldpress.com.au

OUT OF THE SILENCE

THE HISTORY AND MEMORY OF
SOUTH AUSTRALIA'S FRONTIER WARS

Robert Foster and Amanda Nettelbeck

When South Australia was founded in 1836, the British government was pursuing a new approach to the treatment of Aboriginal people, hoping to avoid the violence that marked earlier Australian settlement. The colony's founding Proclamation declared that as British subjects, Aboriginal people would be as much 'under the safeguard of the law as the Colonists themselves, and equally entitled to the privileges of British subjects'. But could colonial governments provide the protection that was promised?

Out of the Silence explores the nature and extent of violence on South Australia's frontiers in light of the foundational promise to provide Aboriginal people with the protection of the law, and the resonances of that history in social memory. What do we find when we compare the history of the frontier with the patterns of how it is remembered and forgotten? And what might this reveal about our understanding of the nation's history and its legacies in the present?

For more information visit www.wakefieldpress.com.au

Wakefield Press is an independent publishing and
distribution company based in Adelaide, South Australia.
We love good stories and publish beautiful books.
To see our full range of books, please visit our website at
www.wakefieldpress.com.au
where all titles are available for purchase.

Find us!

Twitter: www.twitter.com/wakefieldpress
Facebook: www.facebook.com/wakefield.press
Instagram: instagram.com/wakefieldpress